Effective Media Relations

How to Get Results

Third Edition

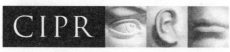

P9-BZJ-525

Michael Bland,
Alison Theaker
& David Wragg

CIPR
CHARTERED INSTITUTE OF PUBLIC RELATIONS

**KOGAN
PAGE**

London and Sterling, VA

First published in 1996
Second edition published in 2000
Third edition published in 2005

Kogan Page Limited
120 Pentonville Road
London N1 9JN
United Kingdom

Kogan Page US
22885 Quicksilver Drive
Sterling VA 20166–2012
USA

© Michael Bland, Alison Theaker and David Wragg, 1996, 2000, 2005

ISBN 0 7494 4380 4

British Library Cataloguing in Publication Data

A CIP record for this book is available from the British Library.

Library of Congress Cataloging-in-Publication Data

Bland, Michael
  Effective media relations : how to get results / Michael Bland, David Wragg, and Alison Theaker. -- 3rd ed.
    p. cm.
  Includes index.
  ISBN 0-7494-4380-4
  1. Public relations. 2. Mass media and business. I. Wragg, David W. II. Theaker, Alison. III. Title.
HD59.B565 2005
791.4502'8--dc22
                        2005005042

Typeset by Jean Cussons Typesetting, Diss, Norfolk
Printed and bound by Creative Print and Design (Wales), Ebbw Vale

Contents

About the authors   *vii*
Foreword   *ix*

Introduction   **1**

PART 1   THE MEDIA CONTEXT

1. **Where and when: a brief media history**   **5**
   Where: origins of the press in Europe   6
   Where: broadcasting in Europe   7

2. **Who: ownership of the media**   **9**
   Personalities and papers   9
   The demise of Fleet Street   11
   Ownership in France and Germany   11
   Cross-media ownership   12
   What now?   13

3. **Media law**   **15**
   Contempt of court   15
   Libel and slander   15
   Codes of conduct   16

Broadcasting codes   17
Time of change   17

4. **Ethics and privacy**   **19**
Regulation   21

5. **Broadcasting in the UK**   **25**
The franchise battle   25
PR in the franchise battle   26
Future of ITV   27
The future of PR in ITV   28
Consequences for the BBC   29

6. **New media technology**   **31**
Radio   31
Satellite television   32
Cable televison   34
Digital broadcasting   35
The internet   36
The death of spin?   37

7. **What is it all for? Media evaluation**   **39**
Methods of evaluation   39
Research   40
Media content analysis   41
Coverage versus content   42

PART 2   DEALING WITH THE PRESS

8. **What: newspapers and periodicals**   **47**
Targeting   47
General press   48
National and regional press   49
Local newspapers   50
Press agencies   51
Consumer periodicals   52
Specialised periodicals   53

9. **Why: press relations – a means to an end** **55**
Matching the media   57
Promoting the product   60
Public relations versus paid-for editorial   64

10.	**News, features and more**	**65**
	News	66
	Timing news	67
	Features	68
	Photographs	69
	A photographic checklist	70
11.	**How: writing for the press**	**73**
	Press releases	73
	Distribution	76
	Features	76
	PR features	77
12.	**How: talking to the press**	**79**
	Jargon	80
	Meeting the press	81
	To lunch or not to lunch?	82
	Press interviews	82
	Press conferences and receptions	83
13.	**Checklist for effective press relations**	**87**
	PART 3 HANDLING THE BROADCAST MEDIA	
14.	**Why: the importance of broadcast coverage**	**93**
	Proactive television	94
15.	**How: preparation and briefing**	**97**
	Asking the questions	97
	Preparing for the interview	102
	Example of a final brief	106
	Checklist	107
16.	**How: winning the interview**	**109**
	A poor interview	110
	A good interview: getting the message across	118
	Checklist	124
17.	**Fine-tuning: handling different interviews**	**127**
	Live	127
	Recorded	128

Panel	128
Down-the-line	128
On site	129
Doorstep	129
Ideas for programmes	130
Contacts with TV stations and people	131
Video news releases	131
18. How: radio interviews	**133**
Radio interview techniques	134
Types of interview	135
Conclusion	*139*
Further reading	*141*
Index	*143*

About the authors

Michael Bland, FCIPR, worked in Germany, Austria and Switzerland as a sales manager for Reuters Limited. After five years in finance and financial journalism he set up and ran the first PR activity for the Institute of Directors and played a key role in putting it on the map. He then spent six years as head of government relations and corporate public affairs for Ford Motor Company Limited before becoming an independent consultant to a number of leading companies and organisations and has trained many thousands of executives in the techniques of public relations, personal presentation, media interviews and crisis and stress management.

Alison Theaker, FCIPR, MA worked in public relations for eight years, in a variety of in-house positions, including: Institute of Housing, National Museum of Photography, Film and Television in Bradford, Metropolitan Borough of Rochdale. She specialises in media relations, internal communications, publications. She was the first member of staff appointed to teach on the new BA Hons in Public Relations at the then Leeds Polytechnic (now Leeds Metropolitan University) in 1990. She became the CIPR's first Head of Education and Training in December 1998. After living in the United States for three years and teaching at Emerson College, Boston, she is now Senior Lecturer at Marjon College, Plymouth.

David Wragg is an independent consultant, living and working in Edinburgh. He is the author of 30 books, including 6 on public relations. Formerly Head of Corporate Communications for the Royal Bank of Scotland, his experience in public relations has extended to transport, travel and the manufacturing industry, as well as financial services. Before entering public relations, he was a journalist, contributing regularly to *The Sunday Telegraph* and *The Spectator*.

Foreword

To the uninformed, public relations is synonymous with press relations and, indeed, many public relations practitioners spend much
of their time dealing with the press. Some spend none of their time
on media relations. The stories that journalists relate of naive practitioners sending the wrong material to the wrong people are
legion. They also frequently, and rightly, complain that press material is badly presented as advertising in disguise and of no interest
at all to them or their readers. The advent of the internet and other
new technologies has meant radical change to the way public relations professionals work with journalists, and more is on the way.
The experts writing here provide a practical insight and guide for
those wanting to work effectively with the media.

In Part One, Alison Theaker deals with the media context.
Knowing something about the history of the media, its ownership
and how it is regulated and being aware of the rules of slander and
libel are absolutely essential. So too is knowledge of the latest
developments.

David Wragg then looks at the written press. He outlines the
opportunities that are available, explains in detail what sort of
approach should be taken and the different types of writing
required. He then provides detailed practical hints and tips on
how to go about it all.

Rounding off the book, Michael Bland takes a behind-the-scenes look at radio and television interviews. He gives an insight into how these media work and then lays down easy-to-follow guidelines on how to get the most from the interview, while also giving the journalists what they want.

By reading this book, the newcomer to public relations practice will have a very solid basis on which to work, will be able to provide a professional service to the press and will gain the satisfaction of knowing they have done their job well.

Anne Gregory
Series Editor

Introduction

For many public relations practitioners much of their time is taken up with media relations. This book aims to inform them about some of the aspects of the media's development which affect their operation today, as well as offering some practical guidelines on how to work with the media successfully.

The media is central to public relations activity for two reasons: the origins of the industry itself in the press agency of such luminaries as Barnum (who coined the phrase 'There's no such thing as bad publicity') and Ivy Leadbetter Lee (who sent the first press release); and the use of the media in the propaganda campaigns during the two world wars in which British public relations was born.

As well as being a powerful tool to persuade, the media can be used to inform relevant sections of the public. With the use of trade and specialist publications as well as the new broadcast media, the public can be targeted narrowly and effectively. The media can be used to encourage two-way communication.

Moreover, editorial coverage carries an implicit endorsement of information and is consequently held to be more believable than advertising, which is paid for and expected to be biased.

By using media relations effectively, public relations practitioners will not only enhance the reputation of their clients or employers, but also themselves, and establish good working relationships with journalists that will serve them well in the future.

Part 1

The media context

Alison Theaker

1

Where and when: a brief media history

In democratic countries the media likes to regard itself as independent and operating in the interests of the general public. The code of conduct of the National Union of Journalists (NUJ) in the UK states that 'A journalist shall at all times defend the principle of the freedom of the press... He/she shall strive to eliminate distortion, news suppression and censorship'.

However, in the 19th century, the press depended on prior intelligence from government of news stories. This information was conditional upon support for that government. There was no investigative journalism. Libel law was used to control content; stamp duty and various taxes attempted to restrict ownership of the press to 'those who would conduct themselves in a responsible manner' (Cresset Pelham, MP), who were, according to Lord Castlereagh, 'men of respectability and property'. Although in 1836, the London readership of the radical press was 2 million (more than that of the legitimate press), by 1837 these papers had disappeared.

The initial capital to start a paper was small. The Leeds-based *Northern Star* was set up in 1837 at a cost of £690, using a hand press and hired type. By 1839 it was making a profit of £13,000, and the break-even circulation was only 6,200. As the Industrial Revolution progressed, printing became more mechanised and so more copies could be produced. But mechanisation also increased set-up costs and break-even circulations considerably: in 1896, the *Daily Mail* cost £15,000 to start and in 1918 *The Express* cost £2 million, with a break-even circulation of 250,000

As the costs and break-even circulations rose, the role of advertising increased. In order to cover costs, newspapers began to aim at the mass market. Working-class papers had large circulations, but little or no advertising. Thus an increase in readership only meant an increase in losses. When the *Daily Herald* was forced to close, it had a circulation of 4.7 million, more than *The Times*, *The Financial Times* and *The Guardian* together. It closed not because people did not want to read it, but because it did not gain enough advertising. Advertisers put their money behind more middle-of-the-road, conservative papers in order to reach the middle and upper classes who had more disposable income. The majority of the press today still support conservative values.

WHERE: ORIGINS OF THE PRESS IN EUROPE

In France, the newspaper industry grew up against the background of the Press Law of 1881, which declared 'the press is free'. Newspapers were regarded as important both for democracy and for entertainment. Before 1870, the *Petit Journal* had a circulation of 300,000, and on the eve of the First World War there were 60 daily papers in Paris and 250 in the provinces. Many papers sprang from political and religious causes. Since the two world wars the number of titles has declined and circulation has stagnated since the 1940s. Recent figures for readership show that the French buy fewer newspapers than other countries in Europe, although café owners may provide free copies for their customers so that readership is rising. Regional papers remain popular.

Three kinds of press grew up in Germany. First, a party-related press emerged after the 1848 revolution, integral in the building up of political parties. Secondly, local papers developed in the provinces which carried both non-political editorial and advertising. Thirdly, the boulevard paper was based in large towns and contained sensationalised stories. One huge press empire emerged in the 1930s under Alfred Hugenberg, whose anti-democratic stance contributed to the downfall of the Weimar Republic. The Nazis took over the German media when they came to power; consequently after the war the Allies created a new press. The British and French set up papers based on a single-party group, while the Americans granted licences to groups representative of a spectrum of opinion. In reaction to this censorship, a variety of newspapers subsequently flourished. As well as national and regional papers, business papers and news magazines, several publications exist which are run by the Protestant and Catholic Churches.

WHERE: BROADCASTING IN EUROPE

United Kingdom

In 1922, the British Broadcasting Company began operations, receiving a Royal Charter in 1926 to become the British Broadcasting Corporation. Its stated mission was to inform, educate and entertain.

The BBC gained a national audience in 1926 with the General Strike. Managing Director John Reith stated that 'the government is acting for the people, so the BBC is for the government'. Statements from strikers and strike-breakers were broadcast, but no representative of organised labour, nor the Leader of the Opposition, Ramsay MacDonald, was allowed to broadcast.

Television broadcasts began in 1936 from Alexandra Palace. Commercial television did not start until 1955, and competition for viewers sectionalised the audience. Although the commercial channel initially struggled to attract viewers, by 1957 Sir Kenneth Clark declared that preference in favour of the new service was 79:21.

France

The broadcast media in France are much more state-controlled than in the UK. Radio broadcasts began in France in 1921, and in 1923 the French state created a monopoly. Permits were sold to private companies for periods of 10 years. Radio was dependent on the government to survive, because, even if the channel were a private one, there would be little or no advertising revenue. France was slow to follow Britain in the adoption of television. There were only 300 TV sets in France in 1939, as against 25,000 in Britain. Complete coverage of the country was not achieved until 1961. The state channel RTF was hampered by frequent strikes, and did not broadcast at weekends. The Director-General of the service was a senior civil servant, and the coverage of demonstrations, particularly about Algeria in 1956, was suppressed. Gerard, the head of radio and TV news in 1961, stated 'A journalist should be French first, objective second'. In 1964 the channel became ORTF, and it included serials, thrillers, comedy and games. In 1975 President Giscard d'Estaing promised no government intervention, and since then relations between government and television eased. Nowadays France 2 and France 3 carry news and documentaries, with the latter being the home of local news. The French/ German collaboration ARTE has a brief to show programmes with a cultural and international flavour.

Germany

In West Germany, Article 5 of the Basic Law passed in 1945 stated that 'freedom of the press and freedom of reporting by radio and film is guaranteed'. Nine regional broadcasting stations were set up, four funded by the United States and one by the French. As the system was devised after the war, there was a resistance to any kind of centralism or uniformity. Broadcasting was and still is therefore controlled by the regional government rather than being a federal responsibility. The first TV channel, ARD, is shared by the nine regional companies, and shows regional programmes in the early evening. Finance is provided through licence fees. ZDF, set up in 1961 to give an objective overall view of world events, also supplements its income from advertising. There are several private commercial stations broadcast by satellite, including RTL and RTL2.

ARD coordinates the nine regional radio broadcasting companies and several commercial stations cover popular music and traffic news.

2

Who: ownership of the media

Since the Second World War, ownership of the media in the UK has become more concentrated. The share of the three leading corporations, News International, Mirror Group and United Newspapers, rose to 74 per cent of daily-paper circulation in 1993.

Ownership of the media carries with it the possibility to influence editorial content, and this has varied with individual proprietors. This chapter includes a brief overview of the main players in the media world.

PERSONALITIES AND PAPERS

In the United States, William Randolph Hearst, immortalised by Orson Welles' portrayal in *Citizen Kane*, epitomised the model of the newspaper proprietor. In 1887 he took over the *San Francisco Examiner*, and over the following 25 years used the paper to make and break political reputations. Hearst himself almost managed to obtain the Democratic presidential nomination in 1904. This link between political ambitions and influencing opinion through media ownership is a common one.

In 19th-century England, proprietors tended to run newspapers for non-commercial reasons. Cobbett's *Political Register* lost millions, and George Newnes lost about £10,000 per year with the *Westminster Press*. Newspaper ownership tended to be concentrated in a few families. Alfred Harmsworth (later Lord Northcliffe) fought as a Unionist candidate in Portsmouth in 1895, but, despite the fact that he had bought a local paper to support him, failed to gain a seat. In 1896 he set up the *Daily Mail*, and in 1903 the *Daily Mirror*. He later sold the *Daily Mirror* to his brother Harold (later Lord Rothermere) in 1914. In 1908 Northcliffe had also bought *The Times* from Colonel Astor, whose brother William Waldorf Astor bought *The Observer* from Northcliffe in 1911. The final member of this group of press barons was Max Aitken, later granted the title Lord Beaverbrook. A Canadian who was MP for Ashton-under-Lyme, Aitken brought the *Daily Express* in order to support Lloyd George against Asquith. He also bought the *Evening Standard* and the *Sunday Express* in 1918.

The *Daily Herald* was the only paper set up as a supporter of the organised labour movement. Begun in 1911 as a strike paper, the TUC owned 49 per cent of the shares. Under editor Julias Elias, later Lord Southwood, circulation rose to 2 million. Owing to a shortfall in advertising, this meant the paper lost £3 million per year, as more copies meant greater losses. However, other papers were forced to follow suit to keep up in the circulation war.

Many newspapers were run like family businesses, with Cecil Harmsworth King, nephew of the founder, taking over the *Daily Mirror*, and Beaverbrook's son Max Aitken at the *Express*. Roy Thomson, another Canadian, bought *The Times*, although he was forced to sell it in 1969 to another newcomer, Australian Rupert Murdoch. Murdoch had also bought the *Daily Herald*, which had been relaunched as *The Sun* in 1964 by King and failed. Murdoch relaunched the paper again, this time with its familiar brash tabloid style, and circulation rose dramatically. Canadian Conrad Black took over *The Daily Telegraph* in 1985, and Czech-born ex-Labour MP Robert Maxwell took over the *Daily Mirror* in 1984.

THE DEMISE OF FLEET STREET

Many restrictive and protective practices had been enforced by the print unions such as extra payments for work not done, and agreed high manning levels filled by 'ghosts', with surplus wages split between those actually working the shift. Power to negotiate had been devolved to individual 'chapels', and proprietors would often make concessions to union demands in order to get the papers produced. Fleet Street losses totalled £21 million in 1975–76.

In the United States, many papers tended to have local monopolies such as the *Los Angeles Times* which attracted 95 per cent of local newspaper advertising. Owners had no fears about suspending circulation in order to achieve the introduction of new technology to reduce costs. Photocomposition, computerised typesetting and web offset printing were introduced. Unlike in the UK, the majority of sales were through subscription, rather than street sales. Thus papers adapted the new technology to the needs of their market with zoned editions and special supplements.

Following this example, the introduction of new technology in the UK began in 1986 with Eddy Shah's *Today*. Between 1986 and 1989 the power of the print unions was broken, mainly through Rupert Murdoch's movement of his production facilities to Wapping. Other papers followed suit, moving to cheaper sites and selling their Fleet Street premises. Computer typesetting, often direct from the journalist to the page, meant greater efficiency but also higher start-up costs and break-even circulations. Although the *News on Sunday*, *Sunday Correspondent* and *London Daily News* invested £6 million, £18 million and £30 million respectively, all failed because of insufficient capital. Only *The Independent* emerged from this period as a successful new title, although subsequently a large stake was sold to Mirror Group Newspapers.

OWNERSHIP IN FRANCE AND GERMANY

Freedom and diversity are enshrined in the French constitution. Between 1945 and 1974, the number of titles declined sharply, from 175 to 75 regional dailies and 31 to 10 Paris papers; and in the 1970s Robert Hersant emerged as a media baron, with ownership of 16 per cent of the total volume of sales.

Media ownership rules in France are structured to stop any single organisation having excessive influence over the media, to ensure diversity. However, in June 2004, the EC allowed Marcel Dassault to buy 82 per cent of the shares of Socpresse, which covers 70 French newspapers, including *Le Figaro*. The company previously was mainly a weapons and aeronautical manufacturer. Another weapons conglomerate, Lagadere, also has interests in the press, publishing and radio. Between them the two companies own 70 per cent of the French press. The International Federation of Journalists has launched a campaign to protest against the concentration of ownership in the French media.

In Germany, there is a similar fear of media concentration. In 1999 the number of independent editorial units for daily newspapers was 135, producing 355 newspapers. Concerns about limiting the encroachment of foreign corporations into the German TV market, such as the purchase of Viva by Viacom, were countered by the problem of limiting foreign investment in German media when the two German media groups Westallgemeine Zeitung (WAZ) and Axel Springer were expanding into Central and Eastern Europe. In fact, the latter gave rise to a Council of Europe sponsored conference in June 2004 in Slovenia on 'Concentration of media ownership and its impact on media freedom and pluralism'.

CROSS-MEDIA OWNERSHIP

Associated Newspapers owns the *Daily Mail*, the *Mail on Sunday* and numerous regional papers and also has interests in Westcountry TV, Classic FM and Great Western Radio in the UK, as well as connections with Herald-Sun TV in Australia and Harmsworth House publications in the United States. EMAP owns 70 consumer magazines and 240 business-to-business titles and exhibitions. It has interests in 19 local radio stations and one digital network. EMAP also owns 44 French titles and claims to reach 50 per cent of the French population every month. News International owns newspapers in the UK (*The Times*, *The Sun*, *News of the World*, *The Sunday Times*), the United States (*Boston Herald*, *New York Post*), Australia (*The Australian*), and the Far East. As well as magazine publishing and film and television interests across the world, one of Murdoch's more controversial holdings was his 50 per cent stake in Sky. He was exempted from the provisions of the 1990 Broadcasting Act so that he could own both newspapers and a substantial part of the monopoly satellite broadcasting company.

The 1995 Green Paper recommended that newspaper groups with less than 20 per cent of national circulation should be allowed to own terrestrial TV stations, exceeding 15 per cent of the television market. Thus groups like Pearson, Associated Newspapers, *The Guardian* and *The Daily Telegraph*, which formed the lobbying organisation British Media Industry Group, would be able to extend their interests into television.

Pressure to grow and expand has resulted in the need to grow and expand internationally. The convergence of media, telecommunications and computer industries enables companies to assemble multimedia networks. This, and the provisions of the Communications Act 2003, will be further examined in Chapter 5.

Cross-media ownership is regulated in the United States by the Federal Communications Commission (FCC). The ownership of a TV station and daily newspaper in the same area is prohibited, in the interests of diversity of viewpoint. The FCC raised the cap on television ownership in June 2003 to allow major conglomerates such as Fox, Viacom and Disney to own TV stations reaching up to 45 per cent of the US population. The rationale given was that this would 'improve the quality and quantity of news available to the public', despite protests that this would lead to fewer independent voices.

WHAT NOW?

Newspapers have invested considerable resources in developing online versions. *The Financial Times* and *The Guardian* in the UK have separate journalistic teams working on the two versions. Tribune in the United States bought Times Mirror, giving the company a total of 60 sites. Some papers give readers the opportunity to exchange views on the news in online chatrooms. The development of new forms of media will be further discussed in Chapter 6.

The costs of setting up printed media forms combined with the pressure to amalgamate in order to compete with the large players can only lead to a concentration of ownership.

There will continue to be a tension between the commercial interests of the media owners and the right of the public to access to a variety of news sources.

3

Media law

CONTEMPT OF COURT

The media may run the risk of breaking the Contempt of Court Act if they comment on active proceedings, jury deliberations, criticise the judiciary or disobey a court order. Any writing, speech or broadcast may be treated as contempt, regardless of intent, but the relevant piece must create a substantial risk of serious impediment or prejudice to particular legal proceedings. Prejudicial media coverage has recently led to the abandonment of several prosecutions. However, the Act also states that publication may not be contempt if part of such a discussion is 'in good faith'. This originally related to an article which *The Sunday Times* wished to publish in 1974 about thalidomide, when civil proceedings were pending on behalf of several children who had been affected by the drug.

LIBEL AND SLANDER

A statement which tends to lower a person in the estimation of 'right-thinking members of society' or which may injure that person in their office, profession or trade, is defamation. The two main types are: *libel*, if the statement is made in a permanent form, such as writing, radio or television; and *slander*, if the statement is transitory, like speech. Every publication constitutes a fresh offence, so that any libel appearing in a newspaper could result in actions against the writer, editor, printer, publisher and distributor.

Jurors have to decide whether the words used were in fact defamatory, in the circumstances. Of course words mean different things to different people. Another problem is changing standards: for instance, a court ruled during the First World War that it was libel to write of someone that he was a German.

Public relations practitioners should bear this in mind when issuing statements to the media, especially those involving competitors. It may also be counterproductive to take legal action in some cases, as McDonald's discovered to their cost in prosecuting two demonstrators for making statements about their practices. The resulting media coverage did more damage than the original statements.

CODES OF CONDUCT

As well as the law, there are also various codes of conduct which apply to the media. The NUJ *Code of Conduct* states that 'A journalist has a duty to maintain the highest professional and ethical standards'. Those who have had experience of tabloid methods may not feel that this code has much effect. Other elements of the code exhort the journalist to strive to eliminate distortion and news suppression, to make sure that information is accurate, to correct any harmful inaccuracies and to protect confidential sources of information. Photographs should only be obtained by straightforward means, and not intrude into grief or distress unless it is in the public interest. Journalists are not to take advantage of confidential information before it is made public, to distort the truth because of advertising considerations or to endorse any commercial product. Mentioning race, colour, creed, illegitimacy, disability, marital status, gender or sexual orientation should only be included where strictly relevant to the story. These considerations should be borne in mind by the public relations practitioner.

The Press Complaints Commission (PCC) is a body set up by the media to regulate its own affairs. The PCC provides an opportunity for injured parties to reply to news coverage. Payment for stories is not permitted, except where the story is in the public interest and payment is necessary for this to happen.

The revised Code of Practice came into effect on 1 June 2004 and still covers such areas as inaccuracy, harassment or the invasion of privacy. However, viewing the statistics on the PCC website, of the 886 complaints made in October 2003 (the most recent month for which statistics were posted) only one was upheld. These codes are only voluntary, and any complaint over inaccurate coverage may raise more problems.

BROADCASTING CODES

If there is misrepresentation on television, there is now one route for redress. The Broadcasting Standards Commission ceased to exist on 29 December 2003, and its areas of concern were taken into Ofcom, the new regulator for the telecommunications industries in the UK. Ofcom covers television, radio and wireless. Its Code of Practice relating to broadcasting follows the same guidelines as that of the BSC, covering avoidance of unfair or unjust treatment and the portrayal of violence and sex. Unlike the BSC, Ofcom imposes a financial penalty on the broadcaster if the complaint is upheld.

TIME OF CHANGE

There are a variety of approaches to media reform. The Campaign for Press and Broadcasting Freedom is concerned about the concentration of the media in the hands of fewer and larger conglomerates (see Chapter 2) as well as restrictions on reporting. They proposed a Freedom of Information Act on the US model, allowing access to government papers; repealing the Contempt of Court and Official Secrets Acts; and replacing the PCC with an independent body which would enforce a general right to reply to inaccurate reporting and monitor press standards.

The Freedom of Information Act received Royal Assent in November 2000, and its access provisions came into force on 1 January 2005. Most authorities have to produce publication schemes of information they hold. The Freedom of Information (Scotland) Act was passed in May 2002. Any individual may make a request to an institution for information, and the request must be dealt with in 20 working days. The Act gives applicants two related rights: to be told whether the institution holds the information, and to receive the information. An individual may also request to inspect records in person.

4

Ethics and privacy

While television is regarded as the most important source of news in Britain, the press is generally held in low esteem. This is especially the case with the tabloid papers. The 1990 Calcutt Committee made some attempts to address the questions of privacy and honesty. Any Government is reluctant to introduce legislation which could be seen as gagging the free press. While reporting is an interpretation of the facts, which involves selection and ordering of the text, there is continuing concern about some of the more sensationalist writing in the tabloids.

The Independent Broadcasting Authority (IBA) Act of 1973 specifically refers to 'due impartiality' in cases of 'political or industrial controversy relating to current public policy'. Impartiality is also enshrined in the BBC's Charter. However, reports of the activities of royalty and politicians in the press over the past years were instrumental in leading to the Calcutt Committee's proposals (see below). The involvement of publicists in the promotion of some obviously untrue stories has reflected poorly on public relations as a profession. For the most part, the publicist is not distinguished in the public's mind from the public relations professional. Cases such as the sale of photographs of the Princess of Wales, taken without her knowledge, to a national tabloid and the invention of affairs between ex-politicians and actresses have caused the reputation of the media to sink even lower.

In Germany, pressure on broadcasters led to the so-called Statutes Movement. Pressure to conform to party-political ideas led Wolf Donner to say: 'It is less a question of concrete cases than of an atmosphere, of an indirect, difficult to prove, anonymous censorship.' Reaction to this movement tended to focus on a perceived (but not demanded) right of journalists to have more say in the content of programmes which they produce. Eventually a much-weakened version of the journalists' demands was introduced, which provided some guarantees of the rights of the individual broadcaster more in keeping with the Basic Law.

In France, radio news has been generally recognised as more impartial than television news, although more people have come to rely on television as their major source of information, as in Britain. Television news has been strictly controlled, with the fair allocation of broadcasting time controlled by an independent commission.

In the United States, there is a significant difference in the behaviour of the media. Because the majority of papers are city or region based rather than national, they are interested in maintaining a relationship with their readers. Also, because of the larger number of graduate journalism courses, journalism has a more academic foundation than in Britain. Journalists rely on the First Amendment: 'Congress shall make no law... abridging the freedom of speech or of the press.'

The Hutchins Commission reported in 1947 and criticised the media for 'meaningless, flatness, distortion and the perpetuation of misunderstanding'. Newspapers have a more serious attitude to corrections, with two-thirds being made within two days of the original error. Apparently the *Boston Globe* once apologised because 'statements made by Sylvester the Cat were erroneously attributed to Daffy Duck'. After the failure of the National News Council in 1973, there have been calls for the media to carry out ethical audits to check the accuracy of their stories. However, more recently there has been concern about the outbreak of 'sleaze' journalism, and the conflicting treatment given to stories in the press and on television. The OJ Simpson trial was a sensational story which was rendered banal by over-exposure. The exhaustive, direct coverage of the court proceedings would have been impossible in Britain.

Recent developments have changed the tone of coverage in the United States. Revelations about journalists manufacturing stories from non-existent sources have been turned into feature films. News coverage since the 9/11 terrorist attack on New York has tended to be very pro-government, with anti-government opinions being denounced as 'un-American'. Michael Moore's film, 'Fahrenheit 9/11', criticised the use of information by the Bush government.

REGULATION

Concerns about press standards have led to discussions about regulation of the media. One of the main concerns has been privacy of the individual, and what constitutes a news story or a gratuitous invasion into someone's private life. In 1989, two Private Member's Bills put forward were concerned with press excesses, a Right of Reply Bill by Tony Worthington and a Privacy Bill by John Browne. Neither Bill succeeded, but pressure for action caused the Calcutt Committee to be set up. This looked at privacy and the press and published its report in 1990. In an attempt to counteract any extreme recommendations, national newspapers appointed ombudsmen to deal with readers' complaints. However, the fact that they were employed by the paper which they were investigating cast doubts on their impartiality. While the committee was preparing its final report, journalists from the *Sunday Sport* infiltrated a hospital ward and interviewed a seriously ill actor, Gordon Kaye, and took pictures of him in his hospital bed. The report and pictures were eventually published, even though Kaye was so ill that he could not recall the interview having taken place. The Court of Appeal lifted an injunction on publication on condition that the paper made it plain that the story had been obtained without consent.

The seven-strong Committee led by David Calcutt QC comprised two lawyers, a journalist, a businesswoman, a professor and an MP. It was unable to prove in any way that standards in the press had significantly declined during the twentieth century. However, both the public and Parliament had a perception that behaviour had worsened. Representations from individuals were heard, as well as from Robert Maxwell, Rupert Murdoch and Kelvin MacKenzie, editor of *The Sun*. The Committee was considering a non-legislative adjudicating body for the press, when the *Sunday Sport* affair occurred. What resulted was that the final recommendations of the Committee did include a last chance for self-regulation, abolishing the Press Council and replacing it with the Press Complaints Commission, but with the proviso that if this did not improve the situation within 18 months then a statutory tribunal should be set up, presided over by a judge. Three new criminal offences were put forward, that could be committed only by journalists: physical intrusion into people's homes; taking photographs by telephoto lens without permission; and trespass. Two possible events were to trigger the introduction of statutory control: the failure of the media to set up the Press Complaints Commission within 12 months; or non-compliance with the Commission's adjudications.

The Press Complaints Commission was set up in January 1991, headed by Lord McGregor, and in the first six months of its existence adjudicated on cases involving Clare Short MP and the *News of the World*, and the *Daily Star* for an article headlined 'Poofters on Parade' about recommendations of a Select Committee that homosexuals should be allowed to serve in the armed forces. However, calls for more controls on press and broadcasters often came from politicians who felt they had been unfairly interrogated, such as Jonathan Aitken MP, who protested about his treatment by John Humphrys of the BBC's *Today* programme.

The Government did not act on the tougher recommendations of the Committee, and the case for or against regulation has not been resolved. In broadcasting, the BBC suffers from the fact that successive governments have sought to influence content according to their political agendas, which has led to it being called both the Baghdad Broadcasting Corporation and the Blair Broadcasting Corporation by MPs offended by particular coverage. The Glasgow Media Unit would argue that both BBC and ITV are pro-establishment.

The publishing of information relating to the activities of some MPs led to recommendations by the Nolan Committee in 1995 that MPs should not be paid for consultancy work. The debate over the declaration of interests goes on, affecting the relationship between MPs and public affairs consultancies and lobbyists.

Whilst the Neill Committee on standards in public life fell short of recommending statutory regulation of lobbyists, both the CIPR and the PRCA (Public Relations Consultants Association) have introduced supplements to their Codes of Practice, and continue to lobby for more controls.

The Hutton Inquiry examined the sequence of events which led to the British Government's decision to go to war with Iraq. The role of Alastair Campbell, the Prime Minister's Communications Director, was examined in relation to information given to the media to disseminate. Attention was focused on whether Campbell had manipulated this information to make the case for war stronger. Whilst he was cleared of exerting 'improper influence' on the drafting of material, questioning of some of his activities and accusations of 'spin' led at least in part to his resignation in August 2003. However, when the full report was published in January 2004, Campbell and the Government were cleared of any wrongdoing and blame was shifted onto the BBC, to such an extent that the Director General, Greg Dyke, was forced to resign.

The Communications Act 2003 again stopped short of formally regulating the media, due to concerns about freedom of the press. The existing five regulators were merged into Ofcom, which was given a remit to cover telecommunications as well. Government proposals to allow newspaper owners to take over Channel 5 were amended to include a 'public interest plurality test'.

Although there is no privacy law in the UK, it was argued that the victory of Naomi Campbell's action against the *Daily Mirror* in May 2004 confirmed privacy principles. 'English law does recognise the right of individuals to the protection of their human anatomy and dignity', said Caroline Kean, a lawyer with Wiggin and Co. Whilst the law lords felt that even those in the public eye have a right to privacy, others felt the judgement would have a serious effect on freedom of the press. This remains to be seen.

Elsewhere in Europe, each country has developed its own national privacy regimes, arising from a fear of a repetition of the use of data to target ethnic groups during the Second World War. The EU Directive on Personal Data was adopted in 1995 to bring them all into line.

5

Broadcasting in the UK

In 1990 the Broadcasting Act set out the conditions under which TV was to operate for the near future. As well as details of how the next round of ITV franchises, to run from 1 January 1993, would be awarded, it confirmed the BBC as the cornerstone of broadcasting in the UK and ensured that both ITV and the BBC would commission 25 per cent of their output from independent production companies.

THE FRANCHISE BATTLE

ITV franchises are initially awarded for ten years, but companies can re-apply after six years for an extension. Franchises were to be awarded to the highest bidder by the Independent Television Commission, but fears that this would lead to mediocrity and lobbying by incumbent franchise holders resulted in a quality threshold being inserted. Bids were submitted in May 1992 and the ITC announced its decision in October. Fifteen regional licences (two in the London area) were awarded in the 14 regions, as well as a national breakfast-television licence.

From the beginning there were major criticisms of the bidding system. All media were scathing about it. Michael Kuhn, part of a group challenging LWT, said that the chances of a new company gaining a franchise from an incumbent was 80:20 against. There were ambiguities about who could bid and the Office of Fair Trading looked at changes to the conditions to avoid monopolies. Originally, companies could not bid for neighbouring franchises.

In formulating bids the pattern of TV advertising had to be estimated for the next 10 to 16 years. This required an educated guess about what effect the penetration of cable and satellite and the launch of Channel 5 during the franchise period would have. Speculation was also rife that with the BBC's Charter up for renewal in 1996, advertising could be allowed on BBC channels.

Mandated hours were set out for news, current affairs, children's and religious programmes. Bidders had to supply evidence of financial stability and technical standards, including details of the facilities they intended to use. Shareholders had to be shown to have commitment and supply credible financial forecasts.

In the resulting decisions, four companies lost their franchises to new challengers. In three areas, Border, Scottish and Central, there were no challengers. Four incumbent companies (Tyne Tees, Anglia, HTV and Yorkshire) retained their franchises by making the highest bid. In Yorkshire's case, their bid was £37 million, as against the nearest competitor with £17 million. Five companies (Channel Islands, LWT, Grampian, Ulster and Granada) retained their franchises despite making lower bids. The ITC based its decisions on whether the applicants would be able to 'maintain [their] proposed service throughout the period for which the licence would be in force'.

Thames and TV-AM lost their franchises to Carlton and Sunrise respectively, who both bid substantially more, but TVS and TSW lost theirs because they bid substantially higher than Meridian and Westcountry TV and were judged to be unrealistic in claiming to be able to maintain this revenue.

PR IN THE FRANCHISE BATTLE

The approaches of a successful incumbent, YTV, and a successful challenger, Meridian, can be compared. YTV linked increased efficiency with an energetic lobbying campaign. Overtime was cut from £9 million to £2 million, and 33 per cent of staff were made redundant. Lobbying was carried out at Westminster and Whitehall stressing the quality of YTV programmes. ITC members were approached to impress them that YTV was a regional company, linked to local charities and running seven regional offices. Local beneficiaries of donations were asked to write to the chair of the ITC, George Russell, to back this up, as well as commercial, industrial and artistic organisations in the region. Poster advertising campaigns were undertaken both in the region and nationally, emphasising the quality of news, drama and comedy produced by YTV. A press campaign promoted YTV programmes and, by a stroke of luck, one of them, *The Darling Buds of May*, obtained the best network slot during the period of the ITC deliberations and gained top ratings. YTV also conducted an intelligence-gathering exercise to find out about competitors and to assess their strengths.

Meridian used a more private strategy, beginning with a campaign for quality TV, and lobbying for the inclusion of the quality threshold. Meridian set up a network of regional PR consultancies to work for them and did not declare the area they were to bid for until two weeks before the deadline. Interest and awareness in the press was raised, and was used in approaching local opinion formers. Favourable press coverage included an article suggesting that most media correspondents considered Meridian to be the most impressive challenger, and that TVS was the incumbent most likely to lose.

FUTURE OF ITV

All incumbents were producer-broadcasters, with their own in-house staff to make programmes. All challengers were publisher-broadcasters, relying on a much smaller core staff, commissioning their programmes from the independent sector. For example, Thames had 1,200 staff as opposed to Carlton's 400. They did not intend to commission in the Channel 4 model, which tends to contract out many one-off programmes, but build up long-term relationships with production houses, commissioning regular series.

The market element of the process emphasised the need for broadcasters to make money. Paul Jackson of Carlton TV said: 'The function of the ITV system is to make programmes people want to watch and get the revenue that comes from it.'

In November 1993, the Government relaxed its rules on ownership of franchises, opening the way for a series of mergers. United News and Media, formerly Meridian, took over Anglia and HTV; Carlton merged with Central and then took over Westcountry; Granada took over the merged Yorkshire/Tyne Tees and LWT; and STV merged with Grampian. Granada and Carlton collaborated on the launch of the digital channel ONdigital in 1998, which cost them well over £1 billion. After being re-branded as ITV Digital in the summer of 2001, it ceased broadcasting in May 2002. Carlton and United News and Media unveiled merger proposals in 1999.

In 2000, Granada bought Anglia, Meridian and HTV from United News and Media, but then had to sell HTV to Carlton to comply with the current regulatory requirements. This created a duopoly of ITV licence holders in England and Wales, which eventually became a single company in January 2004, when Carlton and Granada merged to form ITV plc. The main channel was re-branded as ITV1, although the small, remaining regional broadcasters in Scotland (Scottish Media Group), Northern Ireland (Ulster TV) and the Channel Islands (Channel TV) retain their own individual identities.

Such major changes have resulted in the reduction of the number of transmission centres and substantial job cuts.

THE FUTURE OF PR IN ITV

Most contractors' public relations operations were reduced when the franchises were originally awarded. All four of YTV's press officers were made redundant and publicity was devolved to programme producers. This trend continued with each round of mergers. After the merger of Carlton and Granada into ITV, the corporate communications departments of both were merged and restructured. The Head of Corporate Communications, Susan Donovan, lost her job to Brigitte Trafford from Dow Jones International. Uncertainty about the future of Chief Executive Charles Allen proved unfounded when his restructuring plans reassured shareholders.

CONSEQUENCES FOR THE BBC

In order to retain its Charter, the BBC has to prove that it provides value for money, in an environment of increased competition from a greater number of radio and television services. In its 1992 document *Extending Choice* the BBC set out its purpose: to provide services of 'an unusually high quality that might be at risk in a purely commercial market'. Its original aims to 'inform, educate and entertain' were still included in the document, as well as impartial journalism, extending the range of drama, supporting improving standards of education and reflecting international development and perspectives. The BBC argued that these objectives were best met by 'a broadcasting organisation which offers programmes of quality across all media', and that this should continue to be funded by the licence fee because 'freedom from the commercial pressures to maximise audience ratings and share' was necessary to produce the proposed range of programmes. Increased accountability was offered through better systems for complaint and redress, and the introduction of performance indicators. Other roles currently performed by the BBC, such as an educator and standard setter in the industry (spending £20 million on training) and a cultural patron (supporting five orchestras and commissioning new works from composers and writers) are likely to be affected by an increased emphasis on cost efficiency.

In 1993, the National Heritage Select Committee report supported the continuance of the licence-fee system, praised the BBC's programme quality and affirmed its role in national life.

The Davies review in 1999 examined the way the BBC should be funded in the future, examining how to maintain a public service broadcaster in a competitive market. The BBC must continually show itself to be responsive to viewers' and listeners' needs. The BBC has also set up two websites, BBC Online (bbc.co.uk), which is one of the most successful sites in Europe, and beeb.com, which deals with commercial activities of the BBC. It has also invested considerably in digital technology. Greg Dyke was appointed Director General in 1999, and made many changes to make the BBC more dynamic.

The current Charter runs to the end of 2006, and the Government has already begun the review process. A programme of consultation was launched in December 2003, and opinions were sought from the media industry and the general public. Findings showed that there was still support for the licence fee and for the BBC to remain independent of government and commercial pressures.

6

New media technology

Of course, anything written about new technology is out of date by the time it is printed. Developments in the printed media have been touched on in previous chapters, with the introduction of new printing processes and direct input by journalists which have enabled newspapers to be printed more efficiently and much faster. Heat-set colour instead of photogravure techniques enabled newspapers to produce better colour magazines on ordinary newsprint with a turnaround of four days as opposed to four weeks for a colour supplement on glossy paper. However, the fastest developments are in the broadcast and online media, and it is those that will be examined here.

RADIO

The increase of commercial stations include several nationwide commercial franchises, including Classic FM, Virgin and Talk Radio. Community stations are also growing in number. Community radio has existed for some time elsewhere in Europe, the United States, Canada and Australia, where it has been recognised as providing a local service. The Integrated Systems Digital Network (ISDN) is a digital telephone line which can transmit broadcast-quality audio direct to radio stations, enabling more direct access to programming.

The Broadcasting Act of 1996 allowed the development of digital audio broadcasting (DAB), enabling a wider range of services to be transmitted through the same amount of bandwidth. The first national commercial digital radio services, Digital One, was launched in November 1999. Its principal shareholder was GWR, which did not expect the service to break even for at least five to eight years.

The BBC launched several digital radio services, including a part-time Asian channel. It has also set up BBC Radio 6, carrying classical music. About 60 per cent of the UK receives digital services, and Freeview, the replacement for ITV Digital, carries a number of digital radio stations. RAJAR figures for 2003 showed that Radio 2 is still the most popular station.

SATELLITE TELEVISION

Direct Broadcasting by Satellite (DBS) was first envisaged in 1945 by science-fiction writer Arthur C Clarke, but it was not until 1962 that the first international communications satellite, Telstar, was launched. In 1978, Eutelsat was launched, which was used by the first satellite programmes broadcast from Britain by Satellite TV in 1982 from their studios just off Carnaby Street in London. Because of legislation they could not be received in this country. They broadcast to Norway and Finland, who had relaxed their broadcasting laws, but at that time there were no policies on such broadcasts agreed across Europe. After a year, Rupert Murdoch bought the ailing company and Sky Television was born. Murdoch himself has referred to the development of satellite broadcasting as 'the most important development since Caxton and the printing press'.

At first, Sky was only available through a cable network system which received the signals and broadcast it through cable to a test area of 10,000 homes in the Swindon area. In 1986 the Independent Broadcasting Authority awarded the franchise for satellite broadcasting in the UK to British Satellite Broadcasting (BSB) but stipulated that a high-quality system be used. Known as MAC, or

Multiple Analogue Component system, this was thought to give superior picture quality to the alternative PAL (Phase Alternate Line). BSB had to design and launch its own satellite and was unable to utilise the private Astra satellite, launched in 1988. In 1989, using Astra and PAL, Sky broadcast four channels direct to homes in Britain before BSB had even launched its satellite, and picture quality was found to be adequate after all. The consequent competition between Sky and BSB for the audience resulted in high financial losses for both companies, which led to their eventual merger in 1990 to form British Sky Broadcasting, or BSkyB. This quickly reverted to being called simply 'Sky'.

Sky is in a unique situation in Europe in that it owns the means of distribution, the satellite, and also is a provider of the service, ie Sky Channel. Pay-TV channels, such as Sky Sports 1, 2 and 3 and Sky Moviemax, are also broadcast in this way by using an encoded signal which can only be unscrambled at the user's home by use of a 'smart card'. To receive one of the cards viewers subscribe to the service in addition to the costs of the satellite system.

Channels available tend to be either general entertainment, rebroadcast local services, or specialised or narrowcast services, like CNN (Cable News Network).

International broadcasting is undertaken by Murdoch's Star TV from Singapore, using Asiasat which covers an area from Turkey to Japan. Problems arose in 1989 after pictures of the Tiananmen Square protests and their suppression by the Chinese authorities were broadcast on one of the channels included in the Star package, BBC World Service News. The Chinese government threatened to block Star TV as it could not control the information distributed. In order to keep the lucrative market, Star chose to delete the BBC news from its broadcasts to China. Star TV also broadcasts to India, where local entrepreneurs with satellite dishes took the opportunity to cable their neighbourhoods and set up as small-scale service operators. There are now over 60,000 cable operators in India. India had previously only had a state-controlled monopoly service, Doorshana, which was used basically as a government information channel and was consequently thought to be dull. Star also bought 50 per cent of local station Zee TV in December 1994, a station aimed at the younger end of the market.

Sky now offers over 90 different television packages, including over 200 television and digital radio channels starting at £13.50 per month. It is available to 98 per cent of UK homes and had 7.2 million subscribers as at December 2003. Major competitors are Telewest, ntl and Freeview. Whilst these three all have fewer subscribers, Freeview charges no subscription. Viewers buy a set top box or access it through an integrated digital television.

CABLE TELEVISION

Cable television originally began as a means to transmit terrestrial television channels to those homes which could not receive broadcasts and developed alongside broadcast TV in the 1950s. Now these systems carry other channels and services. Picture quality was originally poor, but was acceptable on the premise that anything was better than nothing. The Federal Communications Commission began to regulate cable in the United States from 1962. Seven towns were selected as pioneers for cable in 1973 in France – Grenoble, Creteil, Cergy-Pontoise, Nice, Chamonix, Rennes and Metz – and the High Audiovisual Council was created.

In 1981, the British government licensed a small number of pay-TV systems in Britain, but originally no advertising or sponsorship was permitted. In 1984 the Cable Authority was established under the Cable and Broadcasting Act to promote, license and regulate the industry. In Europe, Belgium, the Netherlands and Switzerland are the most highly cabled countries. France is the least cabled.

Essentially, cable broadcasts are received by the cable-provider's antenna, and then re-transmitted through fibre-optic or coaxial cable to the homes of subscribers. Other kinds of data can also be transmitted through cable, and one of the most exciting future developments is set to be the introduction of interactive systems, whereby subscribers can watch programmes and select, for example, a camera angle for an action replay. The development and installation of fibre-optic cables, which provide the opportunity for a greater amount of information to be transmitted, will enable companies in future to have direct connections with consumers in their own homes. This will obviously have implications for public relations practitioners in targeting relevant sections of the public.

Approximately 25 companies were granted franchises to set up cable systems to cover virtually the whole of the UK. British Telecom was not permitted to compete for the cable television service at first, but new franchisees were permitted to offer an alternative telephone system to their subscribers. One of the chief advantages for providers of cable systems is that they are able to target areas very directly, with, for example, local news and weather.

The quality of programming on the new variety of channels has been called into question: with so many channels to fill and profits to make, the recycling of old programmes (on channels such as UK Gold) has become commonplace. Other channels, such as CNN, a 24-hour news channel which is also transmitted via satellite, have a high reputation because of their specialist nature. CNN gained much praise for its coverage of the Gulf War, and there was even an instance in 1987 where a remark which President Reagan made about the state of the dollar resulted in the currency coming under attack within 15 minutes of the CNN broadcast. The consequent developments were of course broadcast on CNN within minutes. This illustrates the increased speed of the transmission systems.

To take advantage of the local targeting, Channel One, a cable news service for London, was launched in December 1994. Channel One was owned by Associated Newspapers, and bene-fited from cross-promotional activities in the *Daily Mail*.

Consolidation of licence holders has left Telewest and ntl as the largest players. Both have pursued the development of digital cable services, although in some areas cable franchise holders are still updating their systems. Interactive cable television is the next step, and this is still ongoing.

DIGITAL BROADCASTING

Digital broadcasting involves the compression of information so that, as with digital radio, more can be sent in the same band-width. Quality of picture and sound are improved. At some date, the Government will switch off the current analogue service, enabling the frequencies to be sold to mobile phone companies.

The convergence of companies in the media, computers and telecommunications fields has also led to the development of tele-vision services through the internet.

The increasing number of channels has led to a demand for more material to fill the programme space and an opportunity for PR-led stories, but much of this has been taken up by low-cost repeats and imports. The way to get news onto Sky and other news channels remains the same as ever – by fax and follow-up call.

THE INTERNET

Originally developed in the 1960s by the Pentagon, the internet is a loosely linked system of various computer networks, joined by modems and telephone lines. The US military withdrew from the system when it became obvious that there was not enough data security on the network. JANET (Joint Academic Network) is one of the networks currently available, which as its name suggests links universities and colleges. Communications can be sent to network users all over the world through the use of an e-mail address. E-mail is the most widely used feature on the internet. Letters and other communications can be sent directly to another user's computer, where they are stored until read. Media contact is becoming more common via e-mail, and many journalists like to be contacted in this way. A recent survey found that 91 per cent of journalists prefer to receive copy electronically.

Internet users buy a modem connection, and usually subscribe to a local service provider, who charges them for the lease of international telephone lines supplied by BT or AT&T. After subscription, the cost to users is that of the telephone call. The development of broadband has enabled the provision of 'always on' services, avoiding the delay of a dial-up connection. Broadband services enable faster downloading.

As the telephone system has been updated with fibre-optic cable, so the quality of pictures and graphics which can be sent via the internet has improved. With ISDN (mentioned above) CD-quality audio and video can also be sent. This has applications, for example, in the music business, where interested consumers are able to access video and audio clips of favourite artists' new albums before purchase, as well as detailed information about them. The only limit to this is the time factor involved to download information onto one's own computer, which is extended for graphics, video and music.

The internet is a vast information source. It depends on users browsing through the various information sources available. This has become easier with the development of search engines such as Google, Yahoo and AltaVista. The World Wide Web was developed in the 1990s by European scientists. Pages of information on the web consist of text, graphics and hypertext. The last enables users to highlight words using a computer mouse, and to connect with other linked pages on the internet. Neither the internet nor the World Wide Web are regulated, although some successful prosecutions have been undertaken of providers of pornography sites. It has also become easier to track the senders of malicious viruses, such as the 'I Love You' bug that caused $billions of disruption in May 2000. The virus was found to originate in the Philippines and a suspect was arrested within days. Lawyer Martha Siegel warned: 'PR companies that don't get online will suffer.' However, companies that transgress 'Netiquette' by sending commercial material to users who do not wish to receive it are liable to be 'flamed', or receive a barrage of hate mail. Siegel, with her partner, Cantor, issued a blanket advertisement for their law practice which resulted in 25,000 flames, which not only crashed their own system but that of the server which linked them to the net and several systems in the surrounding area.

Two Ten Communications in the UK was the first to announce a new service to distribute press releases via the internet. Distributing releases in this way avoids clogging up journalists' fax machines with reams of paper, while targeting worldwide. However, some users build in an automatic delete facility for certain kinds of material from certain sources. Releases can also be sent to an incorrectly named e-mail address and miss their target.

THE DEATH OF SPIN?

The CIPR and PRCA formed a joint Internet Commission, and published their findings in a report in April 2000. The report quoted figures that there were then 14 million UK users of the internet, of 190 million worldwide. Subsequently, the *Which?* online internet survey in 2002 put the figure at 19 million UK users. The Commission warned that the development of the internet had led to a new model of communications in which once a message was out, the sender had no control over it. Messages and logos can be taken over and transformed. Pressure groups and those with common interests can set up their own websites with no editorial interference. Individual opinions carry more weight.

Organisations will have to become more transparent and be aware that their employees can pass on information easily.

This is both a huge challenge and an opportunity for PR practitioners. They have become facilitators for employees and other stakeholders, and counsel management on the implications of policy decisions. They have the opportunity to communicate directly with stakeholders without the mediation of the media. Whilst the Commission foresaw that the manipulation of information through so-called spin doctoring would not be viable, so leading to the 'death of spin', the proliferation of information sources and increased speed of dissemination has meant that reputations are ever more vulnerable. Monitoring an organisation's presence on the web is now a necessity for every public relations professional.

7

What is it all for? Media evaluation

Evaluation has been growing in importance in professional public relations. Keith Henshall, CIPR President in 1995, stated: 'For PR to be accepted as a management discipline, evaluation is the key'.

METHODS OF EVALUATION

Traditionally, there were two schools of thought on measuring the success of any public relations activity. The first believed that the results of good PR were intangible and impossible to measure. The second school of thought consisted of those who looked at the number of press cuttings: if these increased, it was good; if these decreased, it was bad.

A variation on the second school was to measure the volume of cuttings against the cost of advertising in the media. This ignored two significant factors. The first was that some media, notably the BBC in the UK, do not carry advertising. The second was the impact of positive editorial coverage, which is always higher than that of advertising.

RESEARCH

Another method which has found favour in recent years is that of scientific research techniques. Before-and-after research can assess the impact of a campaign in terms of the way in which an organisation and its products or activities are viewed by the target audience. This may be extended into regular annual surveys.

Surveys of journalists or investment analysts assess their opinion of an organisation, often expressed in a favour-ability/familiarity chart. A cost-effective way of doing this is to subscribe to the regular research conducted by MORI into the perceptions which business and financial journalists have of companies. MORI provides important indicators of the way in which specialised journalists view a particular sector.

The MORI research is not just a good method of assessing the views of these important opinion formers of the organisation but most especially it shows how they view the press relations activities of companies. Subscribing to the MORI surveys over a period of time can also track peformance of public relations activities.

A specifically commissioned communications audit can focus on those journalists who are known to be of importance to a particular client. It can also be extended so that comparisons are drawn between the company's performance and that of named competitors.

Tracking studies of the corporate image, or regular analyses of audience attitudes, can be helpful in some sensitive fields, such as nuclear energy or pharmaceuticals manufacture. Pre- and post-campaign research is helpful in assessing whether objectives have been attained, but campaigns have to be significant to justify the time, effort and cost of research, which needs to be conducted by an independent and experienced external source.

The research and evaluation debate took on a new impetus in 1999 with the formation of a joint CIPR/PRCA task force on the subject, supported by *PR Week,* which developed it into the Pr%f campaign. This recommended that 10 per cent of the budget of any PR campaign should always be set aside to undertake research and evaluation, and so demonstrate the results of PR activity. A 'toolkit' was published in 1999, which set out practical approaches and guidelines. Case studies were included to illustrate the process and how the value of media evaluation went beyond assessing publicity impact. It reaffirmed that the use of advertising value equivalents (AVE) was essentially flawed. Subsequent editions of the toolkit refined the five-step objective setting, measurement and planning model. The latest edition includes a guide to the variety of media evaluation methods and what they can be used for.

MEDIA CONTENT ANALYSIS

There are a variety of methods of evaluating media coverage. An individual PR practitioner rarely has the time or expertise to carry out detailed analyses, nor the resources to sample all forms of media that might carry messages about their organisation or client. There are many variables to consider. Different publications will have a different impact on the audiences, as will the position and the length of any pieces about an organisation. Most important of all is the question of whether the coverage is favourable or unfavourable, or perhaps somewhere between these two extremes.

Some of the various services available to PR practitioners are now reviewed.

CARMA International

Set up in 1984, CARMA International has offices in the United States, Europe, Canada, Australia, Southeast Asia, Japan and India. CARMA offers customised research to evaluate effectiveness of message retention, how well spokespeople perform, and strength of corporate image. CARMA Full Circle delivers a daily survey of media content. Syndicated and survey research can be added to investigate issues highlighted by media analysis.

Media Measurement Ltd

MML's i-sight product tracks press, radio, television and electronic media coverage. As well as measuring the amount of coverage received, how particular stories develop and which commentators are influential on particular topics, i-sight enables public relations practitioners to track press release performance and to highlight whether certain messages need to be reinforced or redirected.

Echo Research

Combining both traditional and innovative evaluation tools, Echo integrates the results of previously commissioned research with tailored surveys and analyses of client media profiles. A multilingual team can evaluate image and reputation across target audiences and key stakeholders in order to develop measurable targets for PR campaigns and provide global best practice benchmarks. A flexible system enables organisations to build a clearer picture of how they are perceived both internally and externally. Echo carried out an analysis of the image of the PR industry in the media in 1999, as well as more recent surveys on corporate social responsibility.

IMPACON Ltd

The IMPACON process measures the volume of coverage, the number of company or brand namechecks in each item and other variables such as issues or subjects of special interest. All items are given a positive or negative score relating to message and favourableness. In order to ensure objectivity, analysts are not told their clients' identities. Information is converted into tables and charts, and a detailed commentary is added. Reports are available on disk or by e-mail. Costs are related to both the number of cuttings, transcripts and tapes, and the complexity of analysis required.

As well as reading the guide to media evaluation techniques in the CIPR Toolkit (see above), practitioners can also review the offerings of the members of the Association of Media Evaluation Companies (AMEC) on www.amec.org.uk.

COVERAGE VERSUS CONTENT

All the systems available involve at some point an evaluation of the coverage received. However many attributes this process can cope with, a subjective measure of favourability and importance of publication must be made.

It is also possible to use systems such as Dow Jones Interactive or Lexis Nexis to survey an organisation's press coverage. These systems do not place a value on media coverage, and do not provide a favourability rating. One advantage of media content analysis, which considers the quality of coverage as well as the quantity, is that it indirectly takes account of stories which would reflect adversely on the organisation had they appeared.

It also recognises the work of the press office in minimising the impact of bad publicity, and can demonstrate the importance of good issues or crisis-management programmes in terms which company managements will be able to recognise.

It is claimed that public opinion mirrors media coverage and so is one of the best indicators of how companies are perceived. Of course, sometimes life is much simpler.

Small companies with a simple need to generate enquiries may use response rates to assess how worthwhile press relations are to their business.

Even larger organisations can sometimes find that press relations success can be evaluated simply by the impact on business. In one case, a bank using a system of localising press releases to heighten awareness of individual branches had a small four-paragraph news item about a new mortgage product appear in the *Western Morning News*. The product was not being advertised, but within two weeks the branch at Plymouth gained £900,000 of mortgage business.

No system of evaluation is worth paying for unless measurable, specific objectives are first set. This ensures that correct measurement criteria can be agreed. Evaluation must be planned from the start and should be continuous. *Ad hoc* data have only a limited validity and use. Because of the complexity of public relations, the diversity of audiences and the way that PR interacts with other communications disciplines, there is not one simple way of measuring PR effectiveness (Fairchild, 1999).

Media evaluation systems do provide one way of demonstrating results from a major area of PR activity. They work best when used in conjunction with other forms of research, as the majority of the systems reviewed do. The planning and objective setting involved is vital to the practitioner in focusing effort into cost-effective channels. Media evaluation examines the output of media-relations programmes, and by feeding this back into the planning process can inform both strategy and the specific tactics to be used.

Part 2

Dealing with the press

David Wragg

8

What: newspapers and periodicals

While the press has become less important in the eyes of many because of the growth in broadcasting of all kinds and the arrival of online services, it remains vitally important in reaching many audiences and for many messages. In the UK, there are more than 2,000 newspapers.

TARGETING

This wide variety of media provides an opportunity for the public relations practitioner. The wide range of daily and weekly newspapers published outside London enables specific audiences to be targeted on a geographical basis. The many and varied periodicals, most of which deal with specialised interests, mean that people can be reached by their occupations, hobbies or other interests.

By identifying the right publications for employer or client material, public relations can be a cost-effective service. Not pestering journalists who are not interested, not filling up their in-trays or e-mail inboxes with unwanted material, but instead providing specifically targeted and relevant material will improve not only the relationship with the practitioner but also their success rate. It is not simply a case of using the printed word for messages to specialist audiences. Newspapers survive as a significant medium in the age of broadcasting because of the inelasticity of air time. Even a 30-minute broadcast news bulletin will carry fewer items than a tabloid daily paper. A 30-minute news bulletin has an average of just 11 stories each evening, while a quality broadsheet newspaper, such as *The Daily Telegraph*, will have as many on just two pages. Each item broadcast will merit a few sentences, rather than the more extensive coverage afforded by the printed media.

Few countries have such a diverse printed media as the UK. Those countries which have a limited national press and place greater emphasis on regional press include the United States, Germany and Spain. The wide range of specialised publications produced in the UK includes many with a truly international readership, reflecting both widespread use of English and the role of the language as the international language in some industries, such as aviation. This can provide an advantage if a client or employer has a product that needs to be marketed internationally.

The main areas of the press are now reviewed.

GENERAL PRESS

The term 'general press' covers any newspaper that is not aimed at a specialised audience. These newspapers define their audience primarily by their circulation area, which can be wide in the case of the London-based daily and Sunday newspapers. There is also a more subtle breakdown of the audience by class, intellect, political persuasion and, to a lesser extent, degree of affluence.

It is also possible to attribute general press characteristics to some periodicals, such as *Living*, and even those magazines which are aimed mainly at women. This is because their readership covers a wide variety of occupations and interests and is reflected in a varied content, from which the main omission is the absence of news and news-related features. Some include features on personal finance, motoring and travel, as well as those on fashion, health, beauty and home interests which have been their traditional mainstay.

Newspapers do not ignore specialised interests completely. Most have columns given over to motoring, gardening, travel, finance and books, for example. Nevertheless, they do so only to the extent that the general reader with a passing interest in such matters is concerned. The motoring enthusiast will find the general press coverage provides earlier news about developments. A banker will note the news coverage of the general press, but augment it with publications more attuned to his or her specific interests. *The Financial Times* is a hybrid, providing quality financial and business coverage, but also covering other items which one would find in general newspapers, such as political news, motoring and personal finance columns aimed at readers as consumers rather than providers.

For material to be accepted by the newspapers, the editorial team has to be convinced that it will be of interest to a significant proportion of their readers.

NATIONAL AND REGIONAL PRESS

There is a tendency to consider the 'national' press in the UK as being the London-based morning and Sunday newspapers. This overlooks the Edinburgh, Glasgow and Cardiff-based morning and Sunday newspapers which regard themselves as the 'national' press for Scotland and Wales. In Scotland the indigenous newspapers now include the *Scottish Daily Express*, *Scottish Daily Mail*, *Scottish Sun* and *Scottish Daily Mirror*. By contrast, the Belfast newspapers are regarded as regional, because Northern Ireland is a province.

Regional press consists of the morning and the few Sunday newspapers published outside London, Edinburgh, Glasgow and Cardiff; in Scotland it includes the Aberdeen and Dundee morning newspapers. Most regional papers carry international and national news as well as regional and local news, but whenever possible news and features attempt to look at national issues in terms of their impact on the region and, of course, their readers.

Regional morning newspapers usually have an evening newspaper as a stablemate, but there are many cities that have evening newspapers without a morning counterpart. Towns and cities without a morning newspaper but which do have an evening newspaper include Manchester (since *The Guardian* departed that city for London many years ago), Swansea, Bath, Peterborough and York. Although most evening newspapers carry international and national news, their focus is more localised than that of the morning newspapers.

The London newspapers have strong editorial teams which include specialist writers as well as general reporters, and also have their own overseas correspondents in the most important overseas cities. Augmenting the work of their own journalists will be material from the large press agencies.

Regional newspapers with small circulations and limited budgets often will give a single journalist several 'specialisations', although wiser editors endeavour to ensure that these are mutually compatible, such as combining transport and defence, for example, or business and economics, or education and local government. Few have any overseas correspondents, and for this reason such newspapers make much greater use of press agency material. The proprietors of chains of regional newspapers, such as Thomson Regional Newspapers, often provide some material centrally, usually including financial news. Some specialised freelance journalists provide material for several newspapers on a syndicated basis.

The revenue of these newspapers is a combination of advertising and the cover price. Advertising revenue is important to all of them, but especially for the heavier or 'quality' newspapers, where it usually accounts for 75 per cent of revenue when set against their normal cover price.

LOCAL NEWSPAPERS

Most local newspapers are published weekly, although a few appear twice weekly and there are some fortnightly publications. To ensure the economies of scale while maintaining the local links which their readers demand, many local newspapers are published 'in series', so that one newspaper will appear in each of the towns and villages it serves with a distinctive local name, and much of the editorial will be changed to reflect this.

Local newspapers can be divided into the traditional 'paid-for' publications and the more recent 'freesheets', supported entirely by advertising. These are augmented in some areas by community newspapers, sometimes run by volunteers, but sometimes inspired by the local authority. The freesheets will often have much less editorial material than the paid-for newspapers; compared to the 45–55 per cent editorial material of a typical paid-for newspaper, a freesheet may have just 10 per cent editorial, or less.

Local newspapers have very small editorial teams, and even on a paid-for newspaper an editorial staff of six or less is not uncommon. Staffing levels on the freesheets are lower still. While some of the journalists may be able to develop a specialisation, the usual practice is for them to tackle any story which demands attention. In a typical example, on one of the larger and better-staffed local newspapers, a reporter who wanted to develop as a sports reporter was encouraged to do so, but also had to cover a particular district within the paper's circulation area.

Local newspapers place a great reliance on a network of unpaid contributors, who provide news of local events and organisations, and sometimes will even write about a pet interest, such as nature notes or country walks.

Most journalists feel that the great national daily newspapers are the most important. In one sense this is true. A report or an interview in the *Wall Street Journal* may be mentioned in a newspaper or in a broadcast news or current affairs programme. Abroad, overseas broadcasters might refer to the London *Times* or the London *Financial Times*. They would not refer to the *Hobbiton Weekly Advertiser*. On the other hand, many members of the public pay more attention to their local newspapers than to national newspapers and, of course, the local newspaper will often remain in the home all week, until it is replaced by the following week's issue.

PRESS AGENCIES

The Press Association (PA) and Reuters are the major press agencies based in the UK. The PA was founded to provide a service to Britain's newspapers, and was at one time owned by many of them. Traditionally, the PA has been more concerned with UK news and Reuters with international news.

There are two other types of press agency which it is important to be aware of. The first of these is the locally based press or news agency, which provides cover in an area for any newspaper without a presence there. Even the big national newspapers no longer have reporters in every major city, and rely on the local news agencies to fill the gap. National newspapers are not, however, the sole clients of the local agency. Sometimes locally based regional newspapers take their material. At other times, they will be working for regional newspapers in another part of the country. For example, if a Scottish family were involved in an accident while on holiday in the West Country, a local news agency would provide a report and photographs for the newspapers in Scotland.

Locally based news agencies have journalists and press photographers, with the latter often being available for commissions by organisations or PR consultancies. When a photographer who understands the press and the needs of picture editors is required, such agencies are often a good place to look.

The other kind of news agency is the overseas agency with a presence in the UK. If a British story is of interest in the United States, for example, agencies such as UPI or, in the case of a financial story, AP-Dow Jones, will make sure that the relevant US newspapers receive it.

Agencies are interested in news from companies. Local news agencies will be interested in local organisations, while overseas agencies will be interested if the company has business interests in their home country, or has taken a decision which will affect their home country. The larger British agencies are another means of disseminating a message.

All of these agencies work for the newspapers which employ them, not for companies. The exceptions are the news release distribution companies such as Two Ten Communications, which can be used to distribute press releases to the daily and Sunday newspapers. Not every newspaper accepts Two Ten's wire service, and even those that do realise that it is subscriber-driven. Nevertheless, it is a useful support system, especially if a story is being released as quickly as possible.

CONSUMER PERIODICALS

As mentioned, most women's interest magazines, and even others such as the county magazines found in the more affluent rural and suburban areas, can be regarded as part of the general press. Most of these publications are paid-for, although there are a few which are supported entirely by advertising and are delivered free to the residents of affluent suburbs.

True editorial coverage of new products is difficult to achieve in such publications. Providing facilities for a travel writer could result in coverage for a destination or a cruise line, for example. Many of these publications, and especially those handling women's interests, have their editorial content planned far in advance, with deadlines for the Christmas issue often as early as August.

The main obstacle for editorial coverage is that many of these publications either favour advertorial, or use some other form of linkage which means that the advertiser benefits most. Some publications sold in supermarkets have editions for different chains, so that the editorial strongly favours the products sold in the particular supermarket chain.

SPECIALISED PERIODICALS

Specialised publications or periodicals cover a wide variety of activities. They include trade and professional publications and publications concerned with hobbies and interests. Sometimes such publications straddle these different markets, as happens with *Modern Railways* which is read by enthusiasts and by those working in the industry. There are also many academic publications.

The format of such publications can vary from newspaper format through to glossy magazine. The frequency of publication can also vary, from daily in the case of the newspaper *Lloyds List*, through weekly, as with *The Grocer* and *Flight International*, to monthly or quarterly.

Content ranges from weekly publications carrying in-depth specialist content to monthly publications, which sometimes carry news, and sometimes not. The news is often of a specialised nature, such as the number of recent deliveries of railway rolling stock, or the departure of a key figure in an industry.

Most of the directories of the media, such as *PR Planner*, code publications so that news, details of new products, book reviews, appointments, photographs and so on can be targeted. As a rule, any publication which appears less frequently than monthly is unlikely to be interested in news material, and this applies especially to academic publications.

Periodicals can be sold over the counter, paid for by subscription only, be given as one of the benefits of belonging to a club or professional institute, or provided free, with their costs met by their advertising revenue. The variations can encompass more than one of these.

Most have small editorial teams, and augment these efforts by freelance contributions solicited from prominent people within the activity being covered. The best, such as *Flight International* and *The Grocer*, have high editorial standards, and in the case of the former, there is a network of overseas correspondents.

Academic publications will often have a part-time editor, who might be supported by a team of assessors, and the content will often consist of papers contributed by leading academics or researchers. These contributions are seldom paid-for.

Some smaller periodicals are basically one-man bands, and some will be swayed by the opinions of their advertisers. Some will refuse material from companies which do not advertise with them, and this is true of some regional business magazines. It is not uncommon for local chamber of commerce publications to carry news only about their member companies.

Some go as far as one magazine that offered editorial space to anyone willing to pay for it, telling the potential purchaser of this service that the 'editor's right to discard or cut your copy is gone forever'. The problem is that this is a small and specialised market, and so a practice which is likely to result in dull or flabby editorial goes unchallenged by a competitor.

Far more exacting standards are expected in magazines which cover sectors in which there is intense interest, such as aviation. In specialised fields, the number of enthusiasts might have much to do in raising editorial standards and ensuring editorial competitiveness.

9

Why: press relations – a means to an end

There is the story about a British admiral who, in the early years of the twentieth century walked into a gunnery class. Turning to a nervous young midshipman he asked him what was the purpose of gunnery. 'To fire the gun, sir!' was the reply. The admiral's face purpled, and no doubt the midshipman's paled, and he bellowed: 'Boy, the purpose of gunnery is to hit the target!'

Similarly the purpose of press relations is not to issue press releases or handle enquiries from journalists, or even to generate a massive pile of press cuttings. The true purpose of press relations is to enhance the reputation of an organisation and its products, and to influence and inform the target audiences.

Generally, businesses use public relations for a number of specific reasons, and usually in this order of importance:

1. improving company or brand image;
2. higher (and better) media profile;
3. changing the attitudes of target audiences (such as customers);
4. improving relationships with the community;

5. increasing their market share;
6. influencing government policy at local, national or international level;
7. improving communications with investors and their advisers;
8. improving industrial relations.

While media relations seems to come second, in reality all of these objectives can be assisted to some extent by more favourable media coverage. Good editorial comment on a company's financial performance will do more for the confidence of private investors and institutional fund managers than a glossy annual report will ever do. After all, for many investors the annual report is the corporate equivalent of a car brochure, and prospective buyers will be far more interested to know a motoring correspondent's opinion of a particular car.

Even though employee communications programmes are essential, good media coverage will also help to influence employee attitudes. Often many employees will learn most about developments from the newspapers. While employee communications are trusted in good companies, employees still place great store by the judgements of impartial journalists.

Of course, many in business, and in other activities as well, like the idea of press relations for the 'free' publicity it provides. However, good media coverage is not free. This is not because of the growth of advertorial or colour separation charges, but because good-quality PR professionals are seldom cheap. They also need good equipment, and need to spend money on support services.

The quality of press relations is even more important than the quantity. Success may lie sometimes in not having press coverage at all.

In one particular case, a man with a gun entered a public house, threatening customers and staff before he could be cornered by the police and arrested. The press office at the brewery worked hard to persuade the press that there was no need to mention the brewery's name in their reports, and few did. The brewery wished to distance itself from the publicity, and the press generally accepted that the name of the brewery was incidental. Obviously the name of the public house had to be reported.

MATCHING THE MEDIA

Truly effective press relations starts with effective targeting. There is no point in sending a technical story to a general newspaper, or a photograph of a victorious works football team to a periodical which only carries product news. A local weekly newspaper might be interested in the latter story, and the periodical might find the former interesting.

The process of matching a client or employer to the media available is relatively simple. There are four questions to answer:

● What is the function of the organisation?
● Which audiences are essential to its success?
● What messages does it wish to convey?
● Which media are available for this?

Function

An organisation's function will affect its media exposure considerably. In well-diversified companies the press relations demands of operating divisions will vary enormously. High-profile consumer products will require the most support. For example, cruise or package holidays will be on offer to hundreds of thousands of individual customers booking through thousands of travel agents. By contrast, industrial products have far fewer customers, and, depending on the product, these may even be counted in tens rather than hundreds, let alone thousands.

A manufacturer of motor components would have a lower profile and fewer customers to influence than the manufacturer of the end product, the motor car itself. There is more general interest in a new model from a motor car manufacturer than from the manufacturer of commercial vehicles.

Audiences

As well as understanding the organisation's activities, it is important to understand the audience. The holiday example mentioned shows that the traveller is as important as the travel agent. In the case of general cargo operations, the freight forwarder or shipping agent is probably more important than the exporter or importer, but in the case of a large bulk carrier, the broker handling the charter arrangements will need consideration.

The manufacturer of components only needs to reach distributors and the general public if these are sold under the firm's own branding. In many cases, their audience is the small number of motor manufacturers, who will supply the components with their own branding through their own distributors. It is the manufacturer who has to convince the general public, fleet managers and distributors of the worth of the new car. Even then, their distributors usually have a more restrictive link with the motor manufacturer than the travel agent would have with a tour operator, ferry company or cruise line. Commercial vehicle manufacturers also have distributors, but in reaching the purchaser, they may have a limited audience or a very fragmented one, depending on the size of vehicle and its degree of specialisation.

Other audiences are important apart from prospective customers and distributors. Organisations need to influence shareholders, local and central government, and the communities in which they are based, as well as prospective employees and even suppliers.

Messages

Because audiences can be diverse, most organisations will have more than one message to convey. Prospective shareholders will want to be assured about viability, employees about security, and customers about the nature and quality of the product. The old salesman's cliché about 'selling the sizzle and not the steak' also has much truth. The sizzle and aroma of cooking has a greater impact than the sight of a piece of raw meat.

In the case of Carnival cruises, the message could not be simply 'cruise Carnival', still less 'have a cruising holiday'. The message has to convey the benefits of cruising as opposed to other holidays, so the facilities of the ship and the itinerary need emphasis. In contrast, people travelling by ferry are most interested in the route, the schedule and the fares.

Freight forwarders and other agents would be interested in the capacity of a cargo ship, its ability to handle awkward loads, and the schedule.

Travel agents would want the same information as their customers so that they could emphasise the benefits to them. In addition, they would want to know about their own margins, any special incentives, and the availability of the product.

The media

Messages have to be tailored to the wide variety of media available, being clear about the target audience. For example, periodicals which cover the charities field are fine to pass on a worthwhile experience, or air a grievance, but will not help in fund-raising.

If a company is preoccupied with the specialised press, this may be effective in communicating to its peers and distributors, but overlooks the need to attract the attention of decision-makers among the end-users. If a priority was to attract prospective purchasers into the dealers, and to obtain enquiries to be followed up by the sales team, change of media and a different emphasis in press releases and articles or case histories could achieve this. Some media feature reader-enquiry cards, which means that as well as sending prospective purchasers a brochure and the name of the local dealer, the dealer would also receive the enquiry, and pursue it; this would improve the manufacturer's relationship with its dealers.

The key to effective use of the media is to:

● Use the specialised media for the sector to announce developments and air matters of interest.
● Use academic or technical publications to enhance the reputation of staff and to discover if research is being duplicated elsewhere which could lead to collaboration.
● Use other specialised media to interest distributors, such as travel agents or retailers.
● Use the national press to announce major investments, new products if these are of sufficient interest (which in the case of many industrial and consumer products, is very rare), and company results if quoted on the Stock Exchange. Research, campaigns, events and crisis management are other areas to utilise the nationals. Major orders will also interest the nationals – but in this context 'major' means a value of tens of millions of pounds.
● Regional newspapers will often be interested if they can be given the regional angle.

- Local newspapers will be interested in the activities of companies in their area, not least because it affects the prosperity of the neighbourhood. Companies which regard an industrial dispute as nobody's business but their own risk damaging their image among the local community, including prospective employees and potential customers.

The press will usually be more interested in a major issue affecting an industry or a charity, or the results of research which throw light on public attitudes or behaviour than in the straightforward promotion of a product or a campaign. Such material can do much to develop a high level of respect and cooperation with target journalists.

Pressure on newspaper space is often considerable. Newspapers are not elastic. On a busy news day, a story which might otherwise have received extensive coverage in a prominent position will get less space, and stories which might have received a brief mention might have to be passed over.

PROMOTING THE PRODUCT

Genuinely new and different products of interest to the general reader will usually receive the coverage they deserve, and many specialised products will receive coverage in specialist periodicals. Nevertheless, not every product is new and exciting. Many are simply another brand's interpretation of an idea.

Existing products which have remained much the same for many years may also need the use of different techniques to obtain coverage.

Advertorial

Editorial space linked to advertising is often called 'advertorial'. An advertisement of a certain size will result in an agreed amount of editorial being run. Sometimes the newspaper or magazine editor will provide a journalist to write the editorial, but it is more usual for this to be provided by the PR function or consultancy. This crosses a difficult boundary, and many journalists feel it compromises editorial independence.

An advertorial can be a form of paid-for editorial without an accompanying advertisement being placed. Many shopping or restaurant-guide features amount to this. In a local or regional newspaper, a special feature will cover the shopping opportunities in a particular district. The shops and restaurants mentioned are those who have paid for the privilege.

Many regional business publications also allow themselves to be heavily influenced in their editorial judgements by their advertisers. Many will not publish news or features which do not concern their advertisers. This practice has also crept into some regional and national newspapers which will publish special supplements, heavily supported by advertising. Often, the only time a non-advertiser can expect an editorial mention will be if they are responsible for such a major development in their sector that it is impossible for the person editing the supplement to ignore them completely.

There are other occasions when advertorial can be useful. A building society, opening a branch in the suburb of a major city, used advertorial in the two local weekly newspapers. The logic was that the target audience was likely to read these because of their strong circulation in the suburb in question. The advertorial concentrated on the strength of the society and its development, as well as the special features of its products.

Advertorial can help break into the media when genuine editorial interest is low, but professional practitioners will always prefer to win editorial space on the merit of a news story or a background feature, obtaining good coverage after passing objective editorial scrutiny.

Much really depends on the value set by publishers on the quality of their newspapers or periodicals. Appointments columns should be free editorial selected on their news value rather than paid-for advertising – the trend started in Dublin and has spread to the UK, especially Scotland. PR people have generally resisted paying for appointments, which is easy to do since rarely does a new appointment or promotion automatically mean more business enquiries, unlike a new product.

Nevertheless, not all appointments stories are sent to the press by PR departments. The result has been that the appointments columns, especially in Scotland, have ceased to contain stories of the appointment of senior people to Scottish business, and instead have been filled by details of new sales representatives and area managers. No longer do these columns keep the business community abreast of worthwhile changes, but at least anyone interested now knows who to approach for double glazing.

Colour separation charges

Many trade publications will offer to run a colour picture along-side a product story if the costs of separations are paid for by the company. This is a further blurring of the distinction between editorial and advertising which has prompted action by the IPR. At present, colour separations cost between £15 and £70 to produce, but publications have been charging between £50 and £700. The Periodical Publishers' Association guidelines stipulate that the words 'advertisement', 'advertising' or 'promotion' should identify any paid-for editorial space. When illustrations have been paid for, this should also be made clear. The CIPR accepts the case for clearly marked advertorials, but opposes the practice of levying artificial 'colour separation charges' and the like.

The problem is that a colour photograph is more likely to catch the eye of the reader. Nevertheless, this is something which should be resisted.

Newspaper and magazine competitions

Another means of breaking into areas closed to straightforward editorial is the reader competition. Competitions are being used increasingly by motor-car manufacturers. Giving away five or six cars over a week in a daily newspaper can result in extensive coverage, often with the competition mentioned on the front page, and with coverage on the editorial pages. This is more likely to be noticed than advertising, especially if the readers have to collect tokens so that they can enter the competition.

Promotional offers

Special promotional offers, exclusively for the reader of a particular newspaper or magazine, have also become increasingly common in recent years. Often these will also require readers to collect tokens over a period, which has the double benefit of encouraging people to take every issue of the publication, and ensuring that the company behind the special offer receives repeated publicity in each issue.

Many of these offers are self-financing. For example, a restaurant offering two meals for the price of one will do this in the expectation that most customers will also spend on wine and other drinks. For the same reason, free hotel accommodation is usually subject to the condition that all meals are taken in the hotel restaurant.

One cruise operator found that special reader offers were of significance in promoting cruising to a wider audience. A newspaper readers' cruise, in conjunction with a local travel agents, gave the newspaper and the shipping company value, with editorial coverage of local people on holiday. The offer received extensive coverage for several weeks while bookings were being sought.

Readers like to think that they will be going with people from their area or people with similar interests. If members of the editorial team are known to be accompanying the holiday, this is an added attraction, reflecting the often close relationship between many publications and their readership.

Sponsorship

There is a growing use of sponsorship for programmes on independent radio and television. Sponsorship is also becoming more widespread in newspapers and magazines, the difference being that none of the controls exercised over radio and television sponsorship is present in the printed media. Sponsors of broadcast programmes cannot influence the producers' judgement or interfere in editorial decisions, and should not feature in the broadcast. This allows credit-card companies and football-pools promoters to sponsor travel programmes, but the former would not be allowed to sponsor a personal-finance programme (still less one on consumer debt), and the latter would not be able to sponsor a programme on football.

Special editions of some consumer magazines prepared especially for individual supermarket chains are also a form of sponsorship.

Banks sponsor business supplements in regional newspapers, as well as special supplements for certain audiences, such as students. In both cases there is a direct commercial connection.

The practice can influence an editorial and even when it does not, many readers have their perception of the editorial influenced, believing that it is less impartial than it should be.

PUBLIC RELATIONS VERSUS PAID-FOR EDITORIAL

Editorial integrity has become a major issue not only for the media, but for PR practitioners. Editorial coverage is important because people seldom buy publications for the advertising, and the perceived impartiality of the journalists plays an important role in influencing the readers. Paying for coverage may be worthwhile in some cases, if it links to marketing considerations.

During the late 1970s, Cunard threatened to stop advertising cruises in *The Times* and *The Sunday Times* unless its editorial coverage was improved. *The Times* carried the story on the front page as a defiant declaration of editorial independence and integrity. Some at a rival operator had been hinting at a similar strategy before this. Managements, or clients, are always more aware of a competitor's press coverage than of their own! The more coverage people receive, the more they expect, even during quieter periods when their organisation has little worth saying, and even less worth printing.

10

News, features and more

People buy newspapers primarily for their news content. Nevertheless, over the years, newspapers have come to include a selection of articles, more usually referred to as features material, while some periodicals have little or no news content.

Employers and clients will appreciate news coverage presenting them in a good light. Yet successful organisations do not simply make the news, even if it is in a limited way within a specialised field or a confined geographical area. Really successful organisations also feature in articles, whether it be interviews with important members of the management team, a review or critique of a product, which includes much travel writing with the destination as the product, or in a feature on a development within their sector.

Photographs have their part to play. Pictures draw the eye to part of the page as well as simply illustrating a point. Colour provides additional appeal and extra depth. Imagine having to use words alone to describe a new car in such a way that the interested reader would be able to identify it in the street. Photographs of happy, smiling consumers cannot illustrate a mortgage or a life-assurance policy. Nevertheless, even financial institutions make considerable use of photography, using up-to-date photographs of their senior people, of typical branches and historical material. The latter can help to portray the organisation in a certain way showing both a concern for the past as well as the stability and longevity so important in this sphere.

NEWS

Clients or employers often underrate or exaggerate the news value of a development, as they cannot regard it objectively. Modesty can cause people to underestimate the news value of a speech or a paper they are presenting. Objectivity is the most important discipline in assessing news value; superlatives such as 'biggest', 'smallest', 'best', 'first' or 'longest' should be avoided, as should stating a company's product is better than that of a named competitor. Genuine firsts or bests are rare. Even in technical publications, the journalists are rarely in a position to be so sure about such claims themselves, and so, for their own professional credibility, they delete them.

Some journalists will make comparisons of products and recommend the product which they perceive as being best value, especially on the consumer pages of the general press, including the personal-finance columns, while the magazine *Which?* employs teams of testers and researchers. Most publications do not have this type of support.

News implies that something is new, and different. The reason why newspapers are more likely to write about railway delays or road accidents is because on-time arrivals and safe travel are the expected norm. During the early 1970s, when industrial disputes were rife in Britain's ports and hardly a day passed without one or more disputes, the shipping and insurance daily newspaper, *Lloyds List*, once ran a small news item to the effect that there had been no industrial disputes in the Port of Liverpool the previous day! Good news for once, but damaging to the reputation of the port.

News can be:

- a new product;
- an important new contract;

- a senior appointment;
- improved results;
- major investments;
- a major campaign or project;
- research findings;
- an acquisition or a merger;
- a major staff success, perhaps fund-raising for a charity.

Not all of these will have equal weight. Whether or not the general press will be interested will depend on the importance of a new product or a new contract. Money speaks volumes to journalists, because this is an objective measure of the importance of a new contract or a major investment by your employer or client. Newspapers which are regional or local will find news arising in their circulation area to be more relevant.

The appeal to the reader is what matters. A new office desk will be of interest only to specialised periodicals unless, of course, it has some feature which makes it dramatically different from anything which has gone before. A new car from a major manufacturer might have some general news interest, but unless it is extra-special in some way, any significant coverage will have to await its turn in the regular motoring columns. The specialised motoring press would be likely to cover this.

TIMING NEWS

Newspapers have a standard format for each issue. On a quiet news day, a story might be used which on another day would not stand a chance. To some extent this is a matter of luck, but avoid days when a competitor might be making an announcement or when there is some major event, such as the State Opening of Parliament.

Releasing news during periods when the press could be short of stories, such as between Christmas and the New Year, may also be fruitful, but it can also mean that people are not bothering too much with the newspapers then. Timing stories so that they can break over the weekend, ready for Monday morning's newspapers, can be successful, especially for stories concerning the work of charities and for others which may involve the journalists in some additional investigation and reporting of their own, but it will depend for its success on there being a good weekend duty press officer.

FEATURES

Features can support news coverage, providing background on developments, or be part of a regular series, such as motoring, gardening or travel. Features coverage can be a vehicle for advertising.

There are also opportunities for 'think pieces', with prominent people or experts in a particular field writing articles on matters about which they have an authoritative view. In the general press, such pieces are concerned with economics or health matters, and occasionally politics, but in the specialised periodicals, editors may invite contributions from those running businesses which are prominent in their field. The public relations practitioner can ghost such pieces for a client or employer.

Interviews with prominent people often provide good features material (see Chapter 12). Specialised periodicals are often happy to carry features dealing with the progress of a new project or innovation. This can be an invaluable means of keeping a new business development in the press, long after the initial news value has died down.

Features do more than expand the news coverage: they also prolong press interest. It is difficult to maintain the news value of an existing product or service. Production milestones, the millionth passenger to use a service, or major new contracts can maintain interest; but such stories have their limitations.

However, coverage in any regular view or survey is vital. For a company in the holiday business, journalists writing for the travel columns, and those broadcasting on holidays as well, must be aware of the company's products and its latest prices, and also have the opportunity of sampling them. The same goes for companies in other fields, with motor manufacturers getting their share of new car road tests in the motoring columns.

To stimulate coverage in regional and local newspapers, freelance writers with syndicated columns could be invited to test the product. Alternatively, local dealers or distributors could make their test cars available to the motoring writer on the regional or local newspaper.

Some regional and local newspapers also appreciate PR-generated features material, without necessarily expecting it to be accompanied by advertising, on condition that it is not perceived as being a selling piece. Such material can be used to stimulate awareness of the local presence and enhance the image of the local manager as an expert in the field. Unless the features article is about a specific item discovered by the organisation, newspapers may object to references to the company or to its own products in the article. The whole ethos of such articles is that of providing impartial expert advice, and the credit to the organisation comes from being associated with the writer in the byline.

PHOTOGRAPHS

Good photography means photographs which are usable by the press, and which reflect to the advantage of a client or employer.

Marketing-led photography of brochures and advertising usually centres on a product, while newspapers generally prefer action shots. Instead of sterile product shots it will pay dividends to invest in a photographic session with models using the product.

Avoid stereotypes, however. Models do not have to be any particular colour or sex, secretaries do not have to be women, and housework is no longer a female preserve. Members of staff may be used.

Photographs can be tailored to a wider audience by dressing models in white coats for laboratory workers, doctors or veterinary surgeons, brown or blue coats for a warehouse or industrial application, and in suits for a variety of applications.

Newspapers hate the sort of school-photograph line up. People should be in workaday situations which say something about the organisation's activities. This also works with photographs of individuals, such as putting an airline boss into the captain's seat on an aircraft, or having a shipping company chairman on the bridge of a ship.

Checked suits and ties with an intricate pattern may cause problems with colour reproduction. An unusual angle may provide an interesting photograph, such as a heavy load suspended in mid-air.

A good photographer will be able to offer a great deal of invaluable advice on interpreting client needs in a way which is appreciated by newspaper picture editors. Such people also understand the importance of keeping to tight deadlines and are equipped to meet these.

Photographers differ widely, for they specialise. Those whose prime activity consists of wedding photography may not be equipped to provide imaginative architectural shots.

Good photography is not necessarily the most expensive. Several directories list photographers and give details of their specialisations. If photography is needed in a town many miles from headquarters, avoid paying travelling expenses and subsistence: local news and picture agencies are often available for PR commissions.

Media requirements govern whether traditional photographic media or material on CD or transmitted via the internet is most suitable.

Newspaper photographers work quickly and often without supervision. They are accustomed to catching the moment as the VIP steps off the train. Other types of PR photography are more difficult to arrange. Photographs of a new product, the interior of new premises or a group shot of the board will often require time to be spent on lighting, so that not only does everything look good, but disconcerting areas of shadow or reflections are avoided.

Digital photography in many ways has changed all of this – but it has both advantages and dangers. The danger lies in using poor quality equipment since good reproduction requires high definition. The advantages are in the reduced time in processing material, and, if e-mail is used, in distribution as well. Images can be sent to hundreds of recipients within minutes at minimal cost. It is also easier to file and safeguard past images.

A PHOTOGRAPHIC CHECKLIST

There are a few details to bear in mind when commissioning photographs, sending them to the press and maintaining a collection. These include:

● Always caption photographs. With digital photography, put a copy of the caption(s) on the outside of the case containing the CD on which images are stored, while it will avoid confusion if the caption also appears under the image when transmitted or converted into a photograph.

- Keep a record of the photographer with the reference number so re-ordering is simple.
- Obtain special storage files for colour transparencies.
- If black-and-white photographs are needed as well as colour, use black-and-white negative film in addition to colour negatives or transparencies. Many newspapers will accept colour prints but a colour transparency gives better reproduction. Colour printed in black and white is much better today than used to be the case, but a black-and-white print will still be crisper and offer better contrast.
- Good, high-definition colour material can be supplied through the internet or even on a CD, but do ensure that the definition is crisp enough for high-quality reproduction.
- Avoid cheap digital cameras as the definition will not be good enough for reproduction in newspapers or magazines.
- For portrait photographs, black-and-white or colour prints as small as 5 × 4 inches will suffice, but otherwise have a minimum size of 8 × 6 inches or, even better, 10 × 8 inches.
- While the quality of 35 mm transparencies is much improved today, it is still worth considering a larger format if a substantial enlargement is contemplated.
- Always have cardboard-backed envelopes in stock to avoid photographs and transparencies being bent in the post.

Photographers hold the copyright in their work, and it is important to be clear about the cost of subsequent reprints. Some public relations people endeavour to buy the copyright outright when commissioning the photographer, or after they have seen either proof prints or a contact print and can decide which shots they wish to use. If a set of photographs plus a few spares for record purposes for a press release are required, paying the cost of the session and the prints will be less expensive. If varied and extensive use of material is necessary, then it may be worthwhile to buy the copyright.

11

How: writing for the press

Many PR people spend most of their time writing material which is intended for the press, either drafting press releases or writing features material or accurate and interesting photograph captions.

Collaboration may be required to clear some kinds of information before it is sent out. Press releases on new products will be the preserve of the marketing director, although this responsibility might be delegated to a manager in the appropriate department. Releases on a company's annual results will have to be cleared with the chairman, chief executive and finance director.

An agreed decision-making procedure is needed which can authorise press releases quickly, involving as few people as possible.

PRESS RELEASES

Only one press release in ten is published by any newspaper, and the proportion which are accepted by a broad spectrum of the press is lower still.

There are three reasons for this high failure rate:

- A release may not contain news, or if it does, it is so insignificant or so specialised that no one is interested except the issuer.
- Many releases are badly written, include too much technical material and jargon, and hide the real story deep in the body of the release. This is the most common reason for a release failure.
- Many releases are not targeted accurately and are sent with a scatter-gun approach to all contacts on the media list.

Successful press releases follow certain rules:

- A single A4 page is the ideal length.
- Unnecessary and pointless phrases such as 'announces' or 'is pleased to announce' should be avoided.
- Two inches should be left at the top for the newspaper sub-editor to write instructions to the printer and to add a headline. There should be a one-and-a-half inch left-hand margin for the editor's amendments and text should be double-spaced.
- Use e-mail for distribution, so that the story goes straight into the editorial computer.
- Always date the release at the top, so that the news editor can see that the story is current.
- A short, eye-catching headline is needed to attract the attention of a busy news editor.
- The main facts must be included in a short first paragraph. A busy sub-editor will cut from the bottom. The ideal release should still be able to work if only the first paragraph is printed.
- Quotes should be included, attributed to a named senior individual for impact; if the target press are local, the branch manager will be more appropriate.
- Each paragraph should be no more than three sentences, with just one or two for the first paragraph.
- Too much detail detracts from impact, but significant points must be included: accuracy is paramount.
- Good journalistic style is better than legal niceties.
- Jargon should be avoided whenever possible, especially when writing for the general press.
- Superlatives, such as 'best', 'first' or 'excellent', should be avoided.

- A brief concluding statement about the organisation's activities should be included if it is not well known.
- The release should finish with 'ENDS' to avoid confusion.
- A contact name and both daytime and out-of-hours telephone numbers should be included at the foot of the release.
- Several versions of the same release may be provided for different audiences and the publications which reach them. Technical publications might appreciate a longer version of the release, perhaps with a data or specification sheet.
- If a good photograph adds to the story, make sure one is provided, suitably captioned, for those publications which use photographs.
- If a brochure or price list might also help, include it.
- A sample of the product would be useful if it is a practical proposition to offer this. This works well for foodstuffs, and is essential for such items as books, video material and recorded music.
- When a journalist is likely to need time to research and write an important story, allow extra time for this, using an embargo to reduce the chance of the story breaking too early. Head the press release:

'EMBARGO: Not for publication or broadcast before XX.XX hours, XXday, XXdate'.

- Embargoes may need to be flexible. A Sunday-morning story can be allowed in a Saturday-evening newspaper, especially if the story is national and the evening paper is in a town where the company has head offices or a major factory.

An example of the way in which different versions of a press release can work arose when a Scottish firm of investment managers was raising funds for an Oxford college. The story was a UK national story to attract the main body of investors, an Oxford story because of the target, and a Scottish success story because of the company's location. Usually such variations can be handled easily simply by changing the introductory paragraph, but quotes may also need amendment or to be attributed to a different individual.

Attention to such small details will take a little extra time, but will improve the effectiveness of each press release.

DISTRIBUTION

Mailing lists must be kept up to date. Organisations may need several. A bank will need one list for journalists dealing with personal finance, another for those interested in finance for businesses, a third for economics correspondents, and a fourth for its own financial results. Further lists will be needed if it localises press releases to boost the profile of its branches. Other sectors will want to have lists for newspapers read by their customers, for magazines read by their distributors, and so on.

The importance of up-to-date mailing lists cannot be overemphasised. As part of an in-house training session at the Royal Bank of Scotland, the Chief Press Officer asked the business editor of *The Scotsman* for the discarded envelopes from one morning's mail. A large black plastic bin liner was emptied on to a table, covering it with opened envelopes. On inspection most of these were not for the current editorial team on the newspaper; many were not even for their immediate predecessors, and a few were for people who had left five or more years earlier, or even for people who had died.

If organisations persist with one mailing list, every journalist gets everything. Often they will not be interested, and if too few releases are relevant, they will become accustomed to tossing anything from that company or agency into the waste-paper basket. Remember, most journalists prefer to receive press releases via e-mail nowadays.

Creating a website for an organisation, and including recent press releases and photographs that can be easily down-loaded by visitors, is helpful. To ensure that you or your client obtains good value from this, do update the material on offer and try to ensure that it is tailored to meet the needs of different users. Keep the website fresh. Nothing will drive away visitors more quickly than stale news and over-used photographs.

FEATURES

Most features will be written by journalists working either as freelances or as staff members of a particular publication. They will sometimes ask for help when researching a feature, and on occasion they might ask for an interview with someone within the organisation. Such meetings will be covered in Chapter 12.

General rules for the successful handling of enquiries are set out below:

- Information requested must be provided as quickly as possible, and within the deadline set by the journalist.
- Interviews must be arranged speedily.
- Sufficient time must be allowed for the interview. If a journalist wants 20 minutes, it could take twice as long. A good interview will often stimulate discussion on other areas, and perhaps more than one article will result. Sometimes a journalist will need help with background and jargon will need to be interpreted.
- If it is impossible to help within the time set, this should be admitted at once, so that the journalist can go elsewhere and goodwill is maintained.
- If all goes well, the journalist should have everything needed for the article. This may include facts or figures, photographs and back copies of annual reports, and should be provided by the public relations practitioner.
- An offer to check facts and to be available to answer queries should be made. Keep any comments to facts alone, ignoring the style.
- Asking to see the article before it goes to press often causes offence.

PR FEATURES

It is possible to interest journalists in writing an article about an organisation or its work, or an interview with a significant member of the team, but there are many occasions when public relations practitioners are expected to prepare features material. The piece might have a byline, or be unsigned, which happens in many trade publication features. Often, it will be ghost-written on behalf of someone else. The person for whom material is ghosted does not have to be senior, since it could be a feature offered to local newspapers and carrying the name of the company's local branch manager.

The best types of features are those which follow the same rules as the material provided by the publication's own editorial team. The type of material might include:

- reviews of company products or innovations for regular features on the market in trade publications;
- authoritative pieces on developments in the industry or sector ghosted for directors or senior managers;
- advice pieces, which might have the byline of a senior member of the management for general use, but which can be offered to local newspapers as localised pieces carrying the name of the local branch manager;
- review or overview pieces, signed by the company's economist, and offered to the general and specialised press as an alternative to something by one of their own specialists.

The general rules are:

- Always have a start, a middle and an end.
- Always write to the length specified by the editor.
- Most readers will decide whether to continue or move on to another item very quickly, so the first paragraph or two will mark the feature as a success or a failure.
- Unless asked specifically to do so, as in a trade-publication review of products in a certain field, or in advertorial, avoid emphasising the company's own products.
- Be objective when writing about industry developments.
- Always have the material typed in double spacing with a wide left-hand margin.
- Offer to provide material by e-mail, saving editorial time and typesetting costs.
- Provide portrait photographs of the author or product photographs, as appropriate.
- Identify the author's job title.
- Always make sure that the official author is happy with the article: give the author the opportunity to make changes.

When writing advertorial, it should follow the same editorial style as the publication. Do not overbrand. The idea is to produce something that a journalist who is favourable to the product might write and it should appeal to the readers of the publication.

12

How: talking to the press

Contact with journalists is an everyday activity in public relations. Most talking is done over the telephone, but there will be times when this is face to face. Public relations practitioners may also sit in on interviews between your clients or employers and journalists.

The ideal relationship between journalists and public relations practitioners is one based on trust. Efficiency and sensitivity are essential.

The interests of the journalists and the organisation are not necessarily the same. The journalists want facts, information for news items and for feature articles and to have their story accepted by their editor. The organisation wants to be viewed in a good light. Often organisations make the mistake of believing that they can talk to the press only when it suits them, and not at other times. Even if the outcome is likely to be bad news, a willingness to explain will help matters.

Journalists are cynical about those prominent people who are happy to court the press on good days but will ignore it on days when the going gets difficult. Journalists also resent being telephoned or e-mailed to discover whether or not they have received a particular press release.

JARGON

Much of the jargon of journalism has passed into the language. Some of the more common terms are explained below:

- **Quote**. This is what the journalist wants, the opportunity to quote someone, providing their article with additional authority and authenticity. Ideally, they like to attribute the quote to a named individual such as a director or specialist in a particular field, but a spokesperson is second best, and will sometimes be accepted.
- **On the record**. Speaking to a journalist, remarks are automatically 'on the record', unless prefixed by a qualifying remark.
- **Off the record**. This means that whatever is about to be said should not be quoted, and is for the background information of the journalist only. It is important that the intention to go off the record is made clear before making the remarks, and that the journalist agrees to the condition. Remarks cannot be stated as off the record after they have been made, and too much off the record can make an interview useless.
- **Non-attributable**. There are times when someone might be happy to see something reported, but less happy to have their name attributed to the remarks in print. A quote may be attributed to 'industry sources' or 'a senior official'. It may be useful when commenting on a situation affecting an industry sector as a whole, especially if competitors are reluctant to speak. Remarks must be prefixed with this condition, and the journalist must agree, before anyone goes ahead.
- **No comment**. There are still people who believe that this is the right way to address any press enquiry. In practice, it leaves the journalists and their readers to draw their own (usually unfavourable) conclusions. Sometimes comment cannot be made because a matter is *sub judice*, but this must be explained. Customer confidentiality is another example when comment is difficult (see below).
- **Embargo**. See Chapter 11, p 75.

- **Deadline**. The time at which the story must be ready. When a journalist telephones with a question it is important to find out their deadline. Even if information is not available, a phone call should be made before the deadline expires to explain this. There is no need to be too precise in the explanation: saying that an organisation cannot comment on rumours on the stock markets because the finance director has gone to Bolivia, and no one knows when he or she is coming back, might provide a front-page story, and an end to the press officer's career!
- **Scoop**. A genuine scoop, usually billed as an 'exclusive', is rare these days. Giving one journalist a scoop might be worth-while on occasion, but it carries with it the danger of offending rival newspapers.

Customer confidentiality is always a difficult matter. One bank press officer sometimes had this problem when journalists tele-phoned him to discuss a complaint to their newspaper by a customer of the bank. His technique was to explain about customer confidentiality and its importance. He would then offer to discuss the matter fully, and even show the journalist the files, providing that the customer in question provided written permis-sion for the bank to do so. Needless to say, they never did, and the journalist would always drop the story. This technique only works if a complaint to the press is ill-founded. Well-justified complaints were referred to higher management by the press office so that they could be resolved.

Companies negotiating major contracts are often reluctant to say anything worthwhile in advance of the announcement of an agree-ment. When this is happening, it is advisable for the press office to devise a holding statement with those conducting the negotia-tions, so that something worthwhile can be given in response to press enquiries.

MEETING THE PRESS

Good long-term relationships with journalists are invaluable. Journalists differ, and the public relations practitioner must assess those who are to be trusted, and those who are more reckless. For instance, non-attributable and off-the-record quotes should not be offered on first acquaintance.

TO LUNCH OR NOT TO LUNCH?

It has become more difficult to get journalists to attend a lunch simply for the sake of getting to know the press officer, since the pressures on them have grown. Rarely is it worthwhile offering lunch to a general reporter, unless it coincides with an interview with a client or an employer.

The specialised correspondents of the general press and members of the editorial team on specialised periodicals of interest to a client's or employer's activities are a different matter. There are mutual advantages in such meetings as they can tell the press officer their views of the organisation and where they would like to see some improvements. It gives the organisation an insight into outside perceptions and a guide to how to improve press relations in the short term.

It is sometimes possible to arrange lunches where several journalists can meet senior members of the management team. It must be made clear to those being invited that it is nothing more than a 'get to know you' lunch, and that there will be other journalists there. Some will be happy with this, and indeed meeting their peers might be regarded as part of the attraction. Others will express a preference to be lunched on their own, so that they do not have to share any story which arises with their competitors.

Sometimes, managements attempt to 'theme' lunches. This is a good idea if this involves inviting only economics correspondents or the London editors of regional newspapers. It can be a bad idea if it means that the management wishes to talk about a specific subject. Journalists are likely to have their own individual agenda. If the subject is interesting enough to be themed, it does not need to be because the press will be sufficiently interested anyway.

PRESS INTERVIEWS

In arranging interviews, it is important to discover the subjects which the journalist wishes to discuss, and also how much time they will need. Such interviews usually run over the allotted time, especially if they go well. Also, events may affect the subjects covered. If a chief executive has agreed to meet a journalist to discuss the company's plans to develop cross-Channel ferry services and there is a major accident (even to a ship belonging to a competitor) on the previous day, safety instantly comes to the top of the agenda. If there is a major crisis, routine interviews have to be cancelled while the chief executive combats the crisis and fronts a major press conference.

It is important that all press interviews for management and for directors of any organisation have a press officer present. The more senior the individual being interviewed, the more senior the public relations person should be: if it is necessary to intervene, this requires fine judgement and confidence.

The interview can act as a briefing for the public relations function, which is brought up to date on developments and on the organisation's policies and how far it is prepared to commit itself publicly, on or off the record. This makes it easier for the public relations function to comment instantly when the question arises again.

Senior people may not know what is going on at the sharp end and the public relations person might have this information to hand, or can undertake to provide this and any other information that the journalist requires.

If there is disagreement over what was and was not said, the public relations practitioner can remind people what was said when they dispute what appears in print. Usually, such disputes are not worth bothering over.

It should be found out in advance not only the reason for the interview, but whether or not the journalist is familiar with the organisation. It can be useful building in time for a preliminary conversation and having background material ready so that the journalist can be brought up to date on developments.

PRESS CONFERENCES AND RECEPTIONS

Press conferences are ideal for events or announcements of major importance. They are not for trivial matters, and once anyone has acquired the reputation of calling a press conference without real justification for it, they will find that attendance dwindles. These events are not for the vanity of directors or senior management, they are for the press.

Press conferences have the advantage of enabling journalists to question senior management or directors on major announcements or developments, and to ensure that everyone has the same consistent replies. Consistency of message is less likely when journalists are spoken to individually. Timing is another important aspect of press conferences, because they all hear the story at the same time. If 20 journalists were to telephone individually, those at the back of the queue would be short of time to research and write their copy.

Conferences are useful for announcing the results of a large publicly quoted company, or for a major investment or other initiative. They can pull together the organisation's reaction to a crisis or major accident. When possible, a rehearsal within 24 hours before the conference, with the public relations team adopting the role of journalists and challenging statements by those who will be fronting the press conference is a good idea. In the case of a crisis press conference those facing the press must know the current situation.

In the case of a conference for the annual results of a company, investment analysts should be invited before the press so that financial journalists can quote their reactions.

Press receptions can be a useful way of meeting journalists informally, especially if any development does not justify a full-blown press conference. The launch of a new programme of holidays can be an opportunity for travel writers and the travel trade press to be invited to a press reception: it might not justify a press conference.

The main points in organising a press conference or reception are detailed below:

1. Only select and invite those likely to be interested.
2. Let those being invited know the purpose of the event. If many refuse, the event is not worthwhile.
3. Except in a crisis, those invited should be telephoned 24 hours before the event to remind them.
4. All guests should be signed in to provide a record of those attending.
5. Hosts should be kept to the minimum. Anyone who has worked as a journalist will have tales of events where the hosts outnumbered the journalists.
6. Hosts must be briefed on who is attending, and on any likely issues or interests.
7. For press conferences, speakers should rehearse the day before.

8. Only have hosts with a strong sense of purpose.
9. A programme, stating starting and finishing time, is useful. Lunchtime events should end by 2.30 pm, so that busy journalists can get away.
10. Journalists unable to attend should have material distributed at the function sent to them as a courtesy, and for information.
11. Place any statements and photographic material from the press conference on the organisation's website.
12. Timing must be convenient for those being invited. Sunday-newspaper journalists do not work on Mondays. Weekly trade and local newspapers usually go to press on Wednesdays, which is a busy day as a result. Morning-newspaper journalists often start work late in the morning. Evening-newspaper journalists may finish work (especially outside London) by 4 pm.

Clashing with another event should be avoided, especially if run by a competitor. It is not unknown for rival companies to do this: it irritates the press, reduces the impact, and makes the organisers of the second event look silly.

13

Checklist for effective press relations

In order to maintain an effective press relations programme, the following pointers will be useful:

1. Awareness of impending news possibilities affecting a client or employer is vital, including any developments of their own, so that the press office is prepared and can handle the news, be it good or bad, in the most effective way.
2. Media contact lists must be up to date. Contacts are sometimes absent, so editors (such as city, sport, or whatever) should also receive copies.
3. Stories must be angled for different audiences, whether these are identified by their location, interests, age or sex.
4. Deadlines must be kept in mind.
5. A press conference or briefing should only be called when the story is sufficiently important. Directors or senior managers taking the conference must be briefed and, if possible, rehearsed.

6. Seasonal opportunities can be utilised for some products and services.
7. Draft legislation, the Budget and official statistics all provide opportunities for a client or employer to provide comment. The press will favour those organisations able to provide sound, reasoned comment.
8. Research or other insights can be offered to the media to maintain the relationship when other stories are few and far between.
9. Good photographs are important to illustrate appropriate stories.
10. A photographic library of essential items and of people for whom a photograph might be required on demand will improve efficiency.
11. Maintain and keep up to date a good organisation's website – including background material, press releases and features material.
12. Product or service brochures and other explanatory material should be provided if this will help journalists.
13. Ensuring journalists have the opportunity to sample products or services is essential if a review is needed.
14. Embargoes can be used if the media need time to research a story, or if the news needs to break on a particular day; but otherwise they should be avoided.
15. Advance warning can help to improve coverage in the publications which are of most importance to the story.
16. Quotes should be attributed to someone of sufficient authority and interest to the press, and they should be available for interview whenever possible.
17. Ensure that the story reaches the right publications; and do not simply leave it to the post, especially at Christmas or at other public holidays: use couriers, facsimile machines and the wire service or e-mail.
18. Further opportunities such as background articles or features, interviews or photographic opportunities should always be considered.
19. A contact name must be provided on any material sent to the press, including an out-of-hours telephone number.
20. Clashing with major events or announcements by competitors should be avoided, as should busy news days.
21. A photographer should be commissioned for major events, in

case the journalists attending are not accompanied by a press photographer. Only those photographers accustomed to working for the press should be used.

22. Action photographs should be used, which show products at work, using people to provide scale and interest.
23. Racial and gender stereotypes should be avoided when organising photography.
24. Issues that affect an employer or client can provide opportunities for an agreed official reaction.
25. Create a website with relevant material, thinking always of what will interest visitors rather than pandering to corporate vanity. Keep it up to date. Nothing is worse than out-of-date prices, and the same goes for press releases and photographs as well.

Part 3

Handling the Broadcast Media

Michael Bland

14

Why: the importance of broadcast coverage

In the last half-century, television has changed the way we live. It has transformed the way we receive our news and the way our impressions are formed. It has influenced the nature of education... and helped to kill the art of conversation.

Yet all we do is sit there and watch the thing. Too rarely do we go out there and appear on it ourselves: to *use* it rather than *be used* by it.

With more and more stations on more and more channels putting out more and more programmes, there is room on the screen nowadays for almost anybody with something interesting to say.

Yet thousands of business people, leaders of pressure groups, chambers of commerce and fund-raisers go through life assuming that 'TV is for the pros', that they themselves are doing well if they make half a column in the local paper.

Television is a communications medium which is always

searching for entertaining material. Almost anybody can use it to get a message into millions of homes.

For the business person it can be a public relations tool or the death of the business, depending on how it is treated. The same company director who uses other publicity material with the skill of the born salesperson will retreat in terror from a heaven-sent opportunity to display his or her firm or product to a vast clientele through a highly credible medium.

Radio, too, is an invaluable medium, with advantages – and one or two rules – of its own, and most of the important messages about television also apply to radio.

With the TV ad you can use both sound and vision to demonstrate the indispensability of your product. You can *show* how fast your cars go, how kids love eating your breakfast cereal, why people use your deodorant spray.

It's so good that there has to be a catch, and there is: money. Television advertising is expensive in the extreme.

Just one minute of prime networked air time can cost as much as £250,000.

Putting it into perspective, you can buy your own studio equipment, send five executives on one-day courses, have ten days of private training for the top person, pay a year's salary for a television press officer and cost a month's working time for the chief executive, all for the price of *20 seconds* of advertising on a national television programme!

PROACTIVE TELEVISION

They may come to you because they need an expert – preferably an interesting one – to talk about the subject they are covering. Or you may be the perceived or potential 'villain' in a negative story. The stakes are high. Individual and corporate reputations can go down the drain before you can say 'Investigative Journalism'. And we've seen others saved by the skilful handling of a crucial interview.

Of course, there will be the odd occasion when you want to keep a low profile and will have good cause to steer clear of the screen. But in the vast majority of cases when people refuse to go on television, it is on a pretext which boils down to: 'They'll ask a lot of awkward questions and make me look a fool.' And that's the heart of it: 'I might be made to look a fool.' It's understandable, but hardly enterprising.

And there are plenty of other excuses. First, there are the horror stories. We've all seen them: an under-prepared spokesperson dying the death of a thousand cuts in front of 10 million people. Someone campaigning for a good cause is made to look a fanatic by skilful editing. A devoted public servant comes over as a bumbling idiot thanks to some loaded questions. And a businessman who has put his prices up to stay alive is turned into a grasping capitalist by a clever interviewer.

Most of us are uneasy about the alien environment, too. Television studios are so unfamiliar: the lights, the cameras, the trendy people, the clutter, the hassle. Walking into a studio, the average first-timer feels like a missionary entering an Amazon head-hunting village.

Nor do we like being made fools of. For verbal bad eggs and visual rotten tomatoes, television is the hottest thing since the village stocks.

And lastly there's that stomach-vibrating fear of a large audience. Anyone who has been in a school play or had to make a speech knows how he or she goes all to pieces when transfixed by hundreds of eyes.

But successful business is all about seizing opportunities, and television presents a glorious opportunity to promote a product, service or cause.

It's the same story whether the news is good or bad. If it's bad – if they are probing into a strike, a fire, a duff product, excess profits – there's no excuse for absence.

If you refuse to respond you will quite certainly be damned in your absence. Without you there to answer back, the presenters, interviewers, pressure group campaigners and armchair experts will have a field day.

But by having a go you stand at least a chance of putting some or all of the record straight, and of diverting the viewer's attention to another, more positive, aspect of the business. Also, very importantly, TV allows you to show a human face.

Incredibly, however, business people can even run away when it's *good* news. Often a programme which genuinely wants to show a company and its goods in a favourable light has the door slammed in its face by reluctant management who 'don't want a lot of cameras all over the place'.

OK, television is different. We've often seen how people's real personalities are transformed – for better or worse – by being electronically processed and displayed on the screen in two dimensions.

And, whereas a print journalist interviews you for information and subsequently seeks to entertain when he/she writes the copy, a broadcast journalist has to both inform *and* entertain during the interview.

With both print and broadcast media, if you or your message is interesting and entertaining, journalists will be inclined to let you have your say and use what you give them. But when you're not entertaining, when you're pompous, abstract or just plain boring, it starts to go wrong.

The print journalist goes off with your 2,000 words of ramblings and looks for a sexy angle for the readers – and thereby 'gets it all wrong'.

And the television interviewer hears the producer's voice in the earpiece saying, 'God, this is boring, liven it up!' So he or she shoves a pointed stick through the bars and pokes you into 'performing', ie starts to ask some nasty questions and generally duff you up for the entertainment of the viewers.

It helps to understand why they need to do this. Despite their protestations to the contrary, the media are driven by a 'commercial imperative'. If they don't constantly attract people to watch, listen and read, then they will cease to exist. Very quickly. TV producers and interviewers have a constant neurosis that if the viewers find their programme less interesting than the others they will switch over and not come back. Then the viewing figures drop... and the TV or radio people are out of a job.

Thus the driving force behind a broadcast interview – *your* interview – is a couch potato with a zapper and a very short attention span. A depressing thought!

So, except for a small minority of malicious or biased programmes, all that the programme makers want from your interview is 'colour'. And if you don't give them colour *your* way they will get it from you *their* way. And you won't like it.

Now let's look at how to provide it *your* way.

15

How: preparation and briefing

Everyone nods in agreement when told that thorough preparation is essential. Yet almost every disaster on TV and radio is caused by a lack of preparation.

You can – and must – do a great deal to prepare yourself to communicate at your best and avoid being tripped up or making a fool of yourself. Many interviewees who complain of being misrepresented have in fact been guilty of going into the studio with a blind (and seriously misguided) faith that the questions will enable them to communicate their messages – and that's if they actually had any messages to communicate in the first place.

ASKING THE QUESTIONS

The prospective interviewee needs to know the following about the programme he or she is to appear on:

- What is the programme about?
- Why have they picked on this particular interviewee (unless the answer is obvious)?

- What is their source of information? If it is a press cutting, read it beforehand.
- What do they know already?
- What do they want to learn?
- In what context will the contribution be used?
- How long will the contribution be?
- Is it to be live or recorded? If recorded, how much of the interview will actually be used in the final programme?
- Will they be using any film or props?
- Who else is going on the programme (such as a competitor or customer)?
- An idea of the questions would also be helpful.

Consideration needs to be given to the following:

- The exact form of the questions is usually only decided at the last minute, and if the interviewer finds an interesting line of discussion during the programme, it is their job to probe further and forget the original questions.
- The interviewer will have an idea of the sort of questions they want to ask. Television interviewers are professionals. So are their research teams, and they will already be thinking about their line of questioning.
- The line of questioning will give a guide to how the interview will run. If possible, an agreement on the first subject to be covered will help the interview get off to a smooth start.
- 'Playing it by ear' will result in a poor performance. At least half an hour of preparation is ideal. If the request is for an immediate response, a few minutes clarifying the message will pay dividends.
- The purpose of appearing on television is to deliver a planned message or messages, not what the interviewer wants you to say.

Skeleton plan

Say, for example, you are a vegetarian and you have an opportunity to encourage a few million others to become vegetarian too. Your knowledge of the subject is vast. There is a wealth of things that the simple carnivore should be taught – economical vegetarian diets, suffering of animals, cholesterol, flavour and a load of other things.

But now the requirement is to condense all this knowledge into a basic message. At best the speaker will get three points over. And in any case, the viewers or listeners won't remember more than two or three points. These might be:

1. Vegetables are better and cheaper than meat.
2. Meat is high in cholesterol.
3. Animal suffering.

These points should be the basis of everything said during the interview. Whatever the questions, whatever the angle, these points should be stressed.

At this point subsections can be added: for example, point 1 above can be split up:

1. Vegetables are better and cheaper than meat:

   (a) vegetables are half the cost of meat;
   (b) vegetables contain all the protein and nutrients you need;
   (c) vegetables contain roughage and are therefore healthier; and
   (d) you can grow vegetables in your own garden.

Brevity

Years of thinking and millions of words and figures have gone into brief phrases like: 'What's good for General Motors is good for America'; 'There is no such thing as a free lunch'; and 'From each according to his ability, to each according to his needs.' This principle of brevity should be kept in mind when communicating something in a short space of time. On television there is very little time offered, so the punchline must come at the beginning.

Simplicity

The television audience is probably ironing, eating, reading, arguing, putting the kids to bed or thinking of changing channels. Even when the television has their undivided attention they are mentally relaxed and only concentrating at half power. Thus the message must be very simple. For example the Confederation of

British Industry succeeded with a campaign against the National Insurance surcharge largely by calling it 'the jobs tax'.

Repetition

It is better to say the same thing several times (in different ways) than to say several things once. Words and sentences should be short so that everyone knows what is being said.

Impact

Which of the following statements has more impact?

- Animal fats are bad for you and can be fatal.
- A friend of mine died from eating animal fats.

The latter actually gives a picture of someone dying from indulging in non-vegetarian activities.

Which of the following statements would viewers relate to more?

- The new factory will improve local employment.
- Albert Jones bought his friends a drink today for the first time in three years; that's how long he was out of work before this factory was built.

The first one may be shorter, yet it has less impact than the second. *People love stories.* One of the greatest communicators of all time was Jesus Christ. His philosophy is still grasped by hundreds of millions of people in all languages, 2,000 years after his death, partly because he said it all in stories. For example, if he had just told people to have a care for those they did not like, the homily would have been forgotten by morning. So he told them about a Samaritan who took pity on a mugging victim. The message still gets through today.

For instance, the fact that vegetables are half the cost of meat can be illustrated with an example, such as: 'Half a pound of steak costs a fortune. Baked potatoes topped with cheese and celery for all the family costs half what that steak cost.'

Familiarity

Another effective way of communicating is to ring a bell in the other person's mind with something with which he or she is already familiar. Again, Christ was a master at this. How hard is it for a sinner to get into heaven? As hard as it is for a camel to go through the eye of a needle. What better description of a false prophet than a 'ravening wolf dressed as a sheep'?

In talking about a new factory, describing it as 8,000 square metres is difficult to grasp. Could it be put into everyday terms? 'About the size of two football fields' is much more readily understood. Does a reservoir contain 123,455,200 gallons of water or does it hold three weeks' supply for the town? Does a refinery have an unpleasant aroma of sulphur dioxide or does it smell like bad eggs?

Relevance: the 'So what?' test

Finally, go back through everything you intend to say and subject it to the 'So what?' test. It may be terribly important to you... but what about the viewer? If it isn't relevant and interesting to him or her, why are you saying it?

Learn the brief

So far so good. The first part of the preparation time has been spent thinking out:

- why you are going on the programme;
- what is to be said and;
- how to say it.

The interviewee must know the brief so well that a relevant message springs to mind when asked a relevant question. There is a big difference between knowing the message and actually saying it. The interviewee should practise saying the key messages aloud. Be clear about the message, then prepare responses to certain potential questions.

What questions are likely to be asked?

Journalists are only human and there is a finite number of

questions they can ask about anything. A brainstorming session with colleagues will probably give rise to most possible angles. Remember the basic questions: Who? What? Where? How? Why? When?

If the programme is a positive one (eg local news, diary or chat show) most of the questions will be aimed at extracting the good news. Others, especially investigative programmes, will be looking for the negatives.

Likely questions should be listed so that the interviewee is not thrown by the unexpected during the interview. But remember that you aren't going simply to *answer* the questions – you are going to *use* them to put your points across.

Watching different programmes and their different approaches is useful preparation, as is familiarising yourself with the different interviewers. By watching television in an analytical, questioning frame of mind, you can work out for yourself what makes a good or bad interview. When watching a television interview, the following questions can be asked:

- How did he or she get on that programme?
- Is he or she doing a good job?
- What is his or her style of interviewing?
- What are the programme-makers looking for?
- Could I get on that programme?
- How would I set about it?

PREPARING FOR THE INTERVIEW

Before the interview

The moments before a TV interview can be quite nerve-racking.

An ENG (electronic news-gathering) unit – usually a reporter and cameraman plus a single camera or, increasingly, just one person both interviewing and operating the camera – can be disconcerting. But a studio can be even more terrifying with its bright lights, banks of cameras, cables, technicians and many other personnel. The pre-interview period can be used as a warm-up:

Nerves

People worry too much about controlling nerves. If the speaker is genuinely paralysed by them, an acting school can give advice on how to learn a technique such as breathing or the 'squeeze', which inhibits the flow of adrenalin. However, adrenalin can help to produce a good performance.

Some tips to help with nerves:

- Avoid alcohol.
- Avoid nervous, unstructured conversation with anyone who is at hand. Nothing is 'off the record'.
- Ask questions, such as: How much do they know about the subject? How long will the interview run? How much of it are they likely to broadcast? What do they want to ask? Who else are they talking to?
- Don't try to *avoid* nerves – *use* them. You need the adrenalin to be at your sharpest. The time to worry is when you are *not* nervous!

Rehearse

This is the time to rehearse the messages, so that they are in the front of your mind.

Think positive

Psychologically the interviewer has just one major advantage: the fact that he or she is asking the questions. Treat each question not as a *threat* but as an *opportunity* to get one of the key messages across.

Bridging from the questions

By treating the questions as opportunities you will soon get the hang of 'bridging' from what they have asked to what you want to say. It works like this: say one of your messages is that you've just reduced your golf handicap and you want to get this across whatever the question:

Q. Is it true that cholesterol is bad for you?

A. In small amounts, it's probably actually *good* for you – but there's a lot of evidence that if you have too much it can *kill* you. But the negative effects will also depend on your lifestyle, as the right kind of exercise helps to burn it off before it does any damage. My own recipe is golf. By playing twice a week I manage to keep my cholesterol level down and reduce my handicap.

This has (a) answered the question, (b) developed into a 'bridging theme' and (c) moved on to the message. In this case the bridging theme was 'exercise', which was relevant to both cholesterol and golf. It comes easily with practice.

Many if not most of the questions will enable you to respond immediately with the prepared message as it will be directly relevant. If the first question is: 'What's the best way to burn off cholesterol?', golf can be introduced without bridging.

The bar-room interview

Imagine yourself not in a TV studio but in a favourite pub, club or wine bar, chatting with a stranger who starts to ask a few questions about your work, product or cause.

Natural communication involves instinctively leaning forward, looking the questioner in the eye, modulating your voice, using simple language, practical examples and anecdotes, and speaking with enthusiasm and conviction.

Dress and looks

A popular myth has grown up that looks are the most important aspect of a television appearance. This is nonsense. Look at TV for yourself. Who are the people who really jump out of the screen and grab attention? The highly groomed politicians and business leaders? No – it is those who have something interesting to say and who say it with colour and zest.

Obviously, though, loud or scruffy clothes or a sloppy manner or nervous chair-swivelling and fidgeting will detract from the message. The main thing is to feel comfortable in what you are wearing, but there are a few technicalities to bear in mind:

- Stripes or checks, particularly narrow ones, have a stroboscopic effect and appear to be moving.
- Equally disconcerting is flashing jewellery, tie-pins, etc.
- Clashing or really loud colours should be avoided.

- Almost black and off-white are ok (a bit drab, perhaps) but straight black and white looks funereal and disturbs the colour balance of the cameras.
- Interviewees need to check just before going on to avoid stray hair, slipped tie knots and smudged mascara.

Softening up the interviewer

When you start a business negotiation you don't cut straight to the chase. Instead, you soften each other up via casual talk about the weather, transport problems, mutual friends or colleagues, etc.

A media interview is just like a business negotiation: you have your agenda and the interviewer has his or hers. A satisfactory 'deal' is when you have both achieved all or most of your agendas in the 'transaction' (ie, the interview).

So start by showing an interest in the interviewer. They love having their egos massaged. Mention something of theirs that you've seen or heard. Ask about where they come from, how they got into TV or radio, other jobs they've done, how much they know about your subject – and, of course, what they want to ask you in the interview.

Essentially you are getting the interviewer to like you, as it is much harder to be nasty to someone you like. Some casual conversation will also help you to relax.

EXAMPLE OF A FINAL BRIEF

XTV Look Round
Vegetarian interview
Interviewer: Cliff Hanger

1. Vegetables better and cheaper:
   - half the price of meat;
   - all protein requirements;
   - healthier – roughage (example of a fit vegetarian);
   - grow them in own garden (fun!).

2. Why meat is bad:
   - cholesterol (dead friend);
   - impurities (fertiliser poisons);
   - bad for teeth.

3. Ecological:
   - increasing human population (500 new humans born during this interview);
   - decreasing animals;
   - suffering:
     - rearing conditions (describe calf in pen);
     - slaughtering conditions (describe slaughterhouse).

CHECKLIST

PREPARATION

1. Decide whether to do it or not:
   - Who is doing the interview?
   - When?
   - Where?
   - How long will it last?

2. Decide:
   - Is someone available?
   - Is it worth doing?

3. If so ask:
   - Why are they doing this programme?
   - Why pick on this organisation?
   - What is the context?
   - Will it be live or recorded?
   - Any films or props?
   - Who else will be on the programme?
   - What questions will they ask?

4. Prepare – at least half an hour:
   - Plan the message:
     - Maximum three points (distil them; time is short) supported by some sub-points.
     - Use examples.
   - Learn the brief.

5. Anticipate the angle and likely questions.

16

How: winning the interview

Most TV interviews carried out these days are recorded, either at your premises or in a fairly simple studio. But some are still done in large studios, which can be very off-putting with editors, producers, directors, floor managers, researchers and cameramen, not to mention their deputies and assistants all involved in making a big programme. It is fairly safe to assume that the person making the most noise between takes is the producer, while the one making all the noise during takes is the director.

Forget the cameras and look at the interviewer. Looking into the camera during an interview appears contrived, and there is a chance of looking into the wrong camera. A red light on top of the camera lights up when it is on, but even experienced newscasters often play Russian roulette between the red lights. There is no way of knowing when the director will order a different camera to cut in.

Many people use notes or reports as security blankets, arriving at the studio with a great pile of them only to be reduced to a nervous wreck then whey are asked not to take them into the studio. A notepad on the knee can actually give quite a professional look, especially if it conveys the impression of being armed with plenty of facts and figures. The great big golden rule is not to read from them. If the camera catches someone peering at their notes in a frantic search for the answer to the last question, then they will not seem credible to the viewer any more.

A POOR INTERVIEW

Suddenly, it is all about to happen for real. A voice calls out: 'Counting down from five: five, four three...'. Then the interviewer speaks, and the cameras are recording. Let us now create a victim and look at a duff interview. The characters and every aspect of the script are borrowed from what happens in real life – from different interviews at different times, in different words. Though fictional, the interview is certainly not impossible. And a highly controversial – and in reality, indefensible – subject has been chosen to show how even the indefensible can be defended by a skilful interviewee.

We have a typical interviewee – a businessman – and a typical interviewer. A businessman has been selected as one of the vast group of people who are likely to be asked to do an interview, yet who has the least experience in television techniques. But the things we are about to see – the questions, the tricks, the pitfalls, the missed opportunities – apply to everyone.

The story so far

Oscar Winner is chief executive of Basket Eggs, a big poultry and egg producer. The company has announced plans to build a plant at Foxtooth, a town of 100,000 inhabitants. It will be one of the biggest projects in the region, and the local TV station has brought Winner in to be interviewed on the evening current affairs programme.

The interviewer, Susan Sharp, is a seasoned pro. In real life she is a nice woman, with a husband and four children. She feeds the ducks on a Sunday afternoon. But she is a bit cynical about businessmen and if she thinks someone is a baddie or is trying to pull a fast one, she goes in for the kill. She has told Winner about her line of questioning, but has been pretty vague, 'What will the factory do?', 'How much will it cost?', 'Any particular problems?', etc.

Winner, for his part, is completely confident about the interview. There is nothing he does not know about chickens; he is a good after-dinner speaker; and his wife thinks he is handsome. He is so calm about it, in fact, that he got in a quick nine holes at the local golf course before going to the studios.

It is 6.30 pm, and the interview is going out live. Sharp launches into her introduction. The transcript is set out below. Most of the studio directions are omitted for simplicity, and the numbers are inserted for reference when we analyse the interview afterwards. Read it through in one go before going back through the numbers.

SHARP: Our next guest on the programme is someone who has a lot to answer for: He's Oscar Winner [*cut to Winner sitting back* (1) *smiling*] who's to build a poultry plant on the outskirts of Foxtooth. The type of plant planned will be like the one in this film [*film, 45 seconds, showing rearing of chicks and battery conditions, some birds are dying, most losing feathers etc* (2)]. Mr Winner, why are you bringing this kind of thing to Foxtooth?

WINNER: (3) Well, it's a logical decision. The company is expanding and Foxtooth is an ideal location for a new poultry plant. In fact...

SHARP: (4) But we've just seen how senseless suffering is caused to countless thousands of chickens. Why not buy a field here and let them run around more freely?

WINNER: (5) Ah, that simply wouldn't be economical, Susan (6). On a free-range basis you need a square-footage-to-bird ratio of 14.7:1 on grade A feed, and more on lower-quality grain (7).

SHARP: Are you saying that you practically torture helpless birds, simply because it's more profitable that way?

WINNER: Well, it's hardly torture (8). I'm just saying that all the people watching this programme... (9)

SHARP: We all know, (4) though, that your method produces lower-quality eggs. In the film they showed a waste-burning unit: are you going to bring one of those here?

WINNER: (5) Oh yes. That's standard equipment in this sort of plant.

SHARP: But that chimney in the film was belching filthy black smoke over the neighbourhood. Now you're telling us that we're to have a factory chimney polluting the atmosphere (10).

WINNER: Well (11), I should like to reassure the viewers that the chimney will only produce about 120,000 cubic feet of waste smoke per hour [pause] (12). Besides, er... (13) [*pause*] this sort of production requires a certain amount of recycling and waste-burning and so on (14).

SHARP: All the same, 120,000 cubic feet sounds like an awful lot of black smoke for a small town like Foxtooth. Tell me, Mr Winner, how long is the plant going to take to build?

WINNER: Just under a year, we hope, though the first eggs should be in production on a limited scale within nine months. We've got a really good firm on the job, and once it's finished it'll be the most modern plant of its kind.

SHARP: Who's building the plant for you then?

WINNER: I... (15) Why do you want to know? (16)

SHARP: It would be interesting to know if it's a local firm. The construction industry round here has been going through a rough patch lately, hasn't it?

WINNER: Has it? (17) I must admit I'm not using a local firm...

SHARP: Why not?

WINNER: Well, quite simply because we've chosen Stackbricks to do the job.

SHARP: Why Stackbricks, though?

WINNER: Well... I mean... [*angrily*] (18) look, why are you asking me all this stuff about the builders? You're making me sound as though I've been bribed or something! (19)

SHARP: [*coolly*] Ok, so it's a year from now and you've built the factory. What benefit are we going to get out of it?

WINNER: Well, I think (20) the great advantage of the Winner system is that you get more eggs for less money. Everything is automatic so we can cut costs and provide a cheaper egg by the thousand.

SHARP: I see. Do you have enough eggs for export, then?

WINNER: Oh yes! We even sell frozen eggs to China!

SHARP: I'm glad to hear it. That's Mr Oscar Winner, who's going to build a plant here to send eggs to China. What the people of Foxtooth will do for eggs is anybody's guess (21) [*cut*].

That interview took just over two minutes. In that time our friend Mr Winner put his foot in it at least 21 times. Interviewers are not always as tough as Sharp, and interviewees not always as dumb as Winner. But many of those 21 points will crop up even in the kindest interview. Let us go back over it, point by point, and see why Mr Winner did not make it. All the points are important, but five are golden rules (numbers 4, 5, 8, 16 and 20).

1. Look alert

It is terribly tempting to try to relax in a studio chair. This can make someone look too contented, if not a complete slob. It is especially true if the opening gambit is an attack: the camera catches them sitting back, smiling smugly, and the viewer already wants to see the interviewer wipe that silly smile right off their face.

2. Any surprises?

If they are using a film, the interviewee should insist on seeing it first. The same applies to surprise studio guests and any other gimmicks.

3. Shout 'unfair'

If they say it is impossible, or say there is no film and then spring it anyway, the viewer must know right away that the interviewee has not seen it.

4. Do not let the interviewer butt in

In normal conversation people tend to stop when someone butts in. On television the reverse applies. If the interviewer cuts in (without good reason) the interviewee should raise their voice – slightly but firmly – and finish what they were saying. But do not confuse making a point with waffle: the interviewer might be butting in because you have been going on too long! Finish the point then shut up. Twenty seconds is adequate – unless it is something that is both important and interesting (eg a colourful anecdote).

5. Refute incorrect statements

What kind of a question was that? Here Sharp is using a derogatory statement followed by a different question. It is a favourite trick. Politely but firmly step in to correct it, or the accusation will stick.

6. No names

It is a small point, but do not forget that ultimately you are talking to the viewer. Be especially careful of first names. They can make the interview sound a bit contrived or 'pally'.

7. No jargon

That spiel about the 14.7:1 ratio may look ludicrous, but it happens all the time. People are so used to the gobbledegook of their everyday jobs that they forget the viewer cannot understand a word of it. Remember instead the advice in Chapter 15 about using simple analogies. (For example: a space expert in an interview explained the nature and dimensions of a Soyuz space station: 'It fits together like a child's construction set. With the latest addition it's now about the size of a domestic garage.')

8. Do not defend

Somehow on television it is as bad as an admission of guilt. She used the word 'torture': now Winner used the same word again which is just what she wanted. Far from being on the defensive in a television interview, use the offensive – in the nicest possible way!

9. There is only one viewer

He or she is an individual, not 'one' or the 'audience' or the 'viewer'. By speaking to him or her through the interviewer it should not be necessary to refer to them as anyone in particular – just 'you'.

10. Don't let them misinterpret

An interviewer will often paraphrase the message. It is usually done with good intentions to achieve simplicity. But if it is done to the detriment of the speaker, they should put it straight at once.

11. 'Well...'

It is human nature to start with a 'Well...'. It does not do any harm in small doses, but that is the third time Winner has started with 'Well' in five questions. He is losing impact.

12. The calculated pause

The pregnant pause is a device much loved of psychologists and police interrogators. Silence is awkward when in close proximity to a stranger and people feel obliged to fill it. A clever interviewer may sometimes just sit there looking and waiting for the interviewee to say something they may later regret. The interviewer is only too conscious that if the interview is filled with long pauses she will be chewed out by the producer for a boring piece. The onus is on her to keep things flowing. If she clams up suddenly and deliberately, having got over a key point, the interviewee should shut up and wait for the interviewer to crack first.

13. 'Er, um...'

A few 'ums' and 'ers' are normal and ok, but the more they are used the less certain someone sounds about the facts.

14. 'And so on and so forth and the like...'

Meaningless. List your items and quit while you're ahead.

15. He who hesitates

A brief pause for thought is ok, as is meeting a deliberate pregnant pause with silence. But in the wrong circumstances a long pause for thought can look dishonest. And it is also important to keep the interview lively and moving at a good pace.

16. Do not be sidetracked

Interviewers are always looking for a dark alleyway with a corpse at the end of it. (This is one reason for not relying too much on prepared questions and answers.) A good interviewer can sniff trouble a mile away at the end of a sidetrack. The question of who is building the plant is of immense local interest, though you can see that Sharp had not thought of it – she got the lead accidentally from Winner ('We've got a really good firm on the job...').

17. Know your ground

It should go without saying. Interviewers are often backed up by research teams who ply them with facts and figures. Do not make it worse with a dumb retort like 'Has it?'

18. Stay cool

Never get angry. Be firm but polite.

19. Do not volunteer things

Winner has just done exactly what Sharp wanted him to do. Sharp knew she would be in hot water if she made any allegations of corruption, so she has let Winner imply the allegations himself.

20. Be positive

Terms like 'I think', 'It seems that', 'I believe' reduce a firm statement of fact to a personal view. Be assertive. Material should be presented as fact, not opinion.

21. The last word

Another favourite. Under the guise of 'winding up', the interviewer delivers the *coup-de-grâce* while the interviewee sits there open-mouthed and the clock ticks to zero. Do not let them get away with it. Register disagreement at once or silence could be mistaken for acceptance.

The key points

Winner's first and biggest mistake has been saved till now. He went in cold, without a brief. He failed to hammer any key points home – because he did not have any key points to hammer home in the first place. He made the cardinal error of playing the interview by ear because he thought he had all the answers in his head.

Go over Winner's interview and look for the main points he should have got over. He wants to make it clear that Basket Eggs is good news. What are the positive points?

1. For a start, it must be demonstrable that eggs are beneficial or presumably one would not eat them. This is a great time for Winner to be selling his product and to make the viewer want to go out and buy a dozen.
2. A major investment in a plant can be shown to be a benefit to the community. Basket Eggs is sure to provide jobs, to add to the income from rates and to boost local trade.
3. Mass production should make for cheaper eggs: that is good news for the shopper.

Of course, there are other points – those valuable exports to China, for example. But Winner should not concentrate on more than two or three points. The viewer simply cannot absorb any more. Other points can be slipped in if there is time. It is worth noting, from these three points alone, how quickly Sharp's irresistible nasties could be spotted in advance. For example, there are plenty of experts who say eggs are bad for people; there is the fact that a new plant will destroy some piece of greenery; and what about those poor old hens?

In any case Winner should have come to terms long ago with the negative aspects of his business. It would be wrong to pretend that everything is perfect in business, and Winner's line of work is full of warts which it would be both immoral and impractical to hide. His job here is to highlight the positive points and play down the negative ones.

A GOOD INTERVIEW: GETTING THE MESSAGE ACROSS

It is incredibly simple: there is not a question in the world that cannot be turned to an advantage. Every question is nothing more than a peg to hang a case on. There are varying degrees. Some questions are 'gifts'. Most questions, however, require some kind of answer before getting on to one's own material. Only as a very last resort should a question be ignored completely.

Let us say, for example, that Sharp throws in a question about production: 'Just how many eggs a day will your plant produce?' A fair enough question. But Winner's first point had nothing to do with the number of eggs: it was to tell the viewer that eggs are good for you and you should eat more. He knows his plant will produce 50,000 eggs a day: now all he has to do is to add a bit: 'Fifty thousand. That's 50,000 meals. One egg alone has enough protein and vitamins to keep you going for half a day.'

Well, Susan Sharp is a seasoned pro and knows propaganda when she sees it, so she quickly changes tack: 'According to some experts, eggs can cause heart failure – is this what you're advocating?' But Winner has not finished selling his eggs. It would be a mistake to skip the heart-failure problem altogether, so he uses the question: 'Taken to excess, anything causes heart failure. But a couple of eggs a day are really good for you – and they're so versatile. They're delicious boiled, fried, scrambled and in omelettes.'

At the same time, though, many interviewers are getting wise to these bridging techniques. Let us say Sharp asks Winner how much profit he made last year. Winner knows he made a packet. And he knows Sharp knows it. This is a case for a 'perspective' answer:

● 'Last year was an exceptionally good one, but let's get it in perspective. We made £30 million, but eggs are a highly risky

business and with all the money we're putting into the Fox-tooth plant we'll need all the cash we can get.'
- 'It works out at a tenth of a penny per egg.'
- 'At first sight it looks a lot – £50 million pre-tax in fact – but don't forget £20 million of that goes straight to the Government to provide schools, defence and welfare…'

Sharp is only waiting for the figure. The moment Winner says £30 million or £50 million, she will leap in with: '*£30 million!* Here you are making a killing while…' Do not let her get away with it. Keep talking and insist on making the point.

Now it is time to apply the lessons to Winner's first interview. The story is the same. The people are the same, and to demonstrate how Winner should have dealt with each question, the questions are the same:

SHARP: Our next guest on the programme is someone who has a lot to answer for. He's Oscar Winner [*cut to Winner, sitting up, intent and alert!*] who's to build a poultry plant on the outskirts of Foxtooth. The type of plant planned is to be like the one in this film [*film, 45 seconds, showing rearing of chicks and battery conditions, some birds dying, most losing feathers, etc*]. Mr Winner, why are you bringing this kind of thing to Foxtooth?

WINNER: (1) If you'd shown me the film before the programme I could have told you how out of date it was. It completely failed to show the immense improvement in the standards of egg produc-tion in the last few years. (2) The Foxtooth plant…

SHARP: But we've just seen…

WINNER: (3) [*more firmly*] The Foxtooth plant will give a vital boost to what is probably the most important area of food produc-tion today (4).

SHARP: But we've just seen how senseless suffering is caused to countless thousands of chickens. Why not buy a field here and let them run around a bit?

WINNER: If you'd shown film of a field of chickens you'd have seen why (5). Next time you see a flock of free-range chickens, just watch them for a while. Their life is hell. You'll see that a few strong birds peck the others into a state where they're so miserable that they lay far fewer eggs than their protected sisters in a battery plant (6).

SHARP: Are you saying that you practically torture helpless birds, simply because it's more profitable that way?

WINNER: (7) All the evidence points to the fact that our hens have a safer and longer life and lay more eggs (8). We can check them the whole time so we know that every egg which leaves our plant is good and wholesome.

SHARP: We all know, though, that your method produces lower-quality eggs. In the film they showed a waste-burning unit: are you going to bring one of these here?

WINNER: (9) Listen, our eggs have been tested side by side with free-range eggs and they are every bit as good. Do you realise that there are more proteins and nutrients in one single egg than in any other foodstuff at the price? (10)

SHARP: What about this waste-burning unit?

WINNER: Either you have a pile of chicken feathers a mile high or you process them (11). As a matter of fact our process has a number of useful side products – manure, chicken paste, offal (12).

SHARP: But that chimney in the film was belching filthy black smoke over the neighbourhood. Now you're telling us that we're to have a factory chimney polluting the atmosphere.

WINNER: I'm telling you the exact opposite. It will produce no more smoke than half a dozen domestic chimneys (13) – and only occasionally at that.

SHARP: Tell me, Mr Winner, how long is the plant going to take to build?

WINNER: The sooner the better as far as everyone's concerned! When this plant is in production it'll mean 200 new jobs for

Foxtooth (14). It's the biggest industrial investment in this region for years.

SHARP: Who's building the plant for you then?

WINNER: (15) It's important first to look at the scope of the project. These new buildings will be the most up to date, safe and efficient in the world. We're investing a fortune to produce the best eggs at the lowest price.

SHARP: But it would be interesting to know if it's a local firm. The construction industry round here has been going through a rough patch lately, hasn't it?

WINNER: (16) It has everywhere, I'm afraid, and of course we looked at the local building firms when we tendered. In this case we chose Stackbricks because of their experience of building this sort of plant. Next time you're in the Ducktown region take a look at the big, modern egg farm they built there... (17)

SHARP: Ok, so it's a year from now and you've built the factory. What benefit are we going to get out of it? (18)

WINNER: (19) The biggest single benefit is that you'll get more eggs for less money. Everything is automatic so we can cut costs and give you a cheaper egg.

SHARP: I see. Do you have enough eggs for export, then?

WINNER: Oh yes! We even sell frozen eggs to China.

SHARP: I'm glad to hear it. That's Mr Oscar Winner, who says he's going to build a plant here to send eggs to China. Meanwhile, I wonder what the people of Foxtooth will do for eggs.

WINNER: (20) They come first, of course... [*cut*].

That's more like it

There is no such thing as a perfect interview, but this time Winner made a good showing by applying some elementary techniques.

With the same story and basically the same questions he got his key points over and dealt firmly with the nasty questions. What's more, Sharp and her bosses will be pleased with this more lively and informative interview, so the odds have improved on Winner being invited back for another go – when the factory opens, for example.

It is worth a look back over the interview to examine the ways Winner improved. This time he scored 20 times. We will just run over the inserted numbers and see what lessons he learnt:

1. He is making it clear to the viewer, right from the start, that he has not been given a chance to see the film. Not only does this stop him making a fool of himself, but it also encourages the viewer to side with Winner over this unfair treatment.
2. Then he immediately uses the unseen film as a bridge to stress the improvements in egg production.
3. No nonsense. He had not finished speaking so he beat Sharp at her own game and cut in. Note that he does so firmly rather than aggressively.
4. At the start of the interview, Winner has now got two points in already. He has used the 'improvements' bit as a peg for reminding the viewer that eggs are an important food product.
5. In the first interview he was on the defensive over this 'suffering' accusation. This time he attacks by comparing it with the alleged greater suffering of free-range chickens.
6. Now he is telling a story – painting a picture for the viewer of a lot of chickens giving each other a rough time.
7. Sharp will not give in on her 'suffering' angle. So Winner uses it to reiterate his view that his chickens are happier.
8. He also realises, though, that Sharp is starting to sidetrack him with this angle. So, before Sharp can get started again, Winner bangs in another key point on the back of his 'happy hens' argument. He is starting to make the viewer feel like eating an egg.
9. This is the nearest he gets to showing anger. Underneath he is furious at Sharp's sniping, but that 'listen...' is firm not angry, and he is really telling the viewer: 'listen to me, not her.'
10. Again he uses the moment to sell a few more eggs.

11. It does not take much imagination to convert a simple reassurance about a waste-burning unit into an image in the viewer's mind of a pile of chicken feathers a mile high. Yet it doubles the impact.

12. 'And while we're on the subject of the waste-burner', Winner says in effect: 'Look at all the goodies you are going to get out of my factory.' His plug for chicken paste does not really have much to do with the waste-burner, but it only takes a few words to link the two.

13. Here is a good example of an analogy. Gone are the 120,000 cubic feet and in their place are half a dozen domestic chimneys – which the viewer can picture at once.

14. It has taken a couple of minutes for Winner to have a chance to get his key point in, but he is not going to let it go. Again, he uses the question as a bridge. If he merely answers the question 'How long is it going to take to build?', he will never demonstrate the boost he is giving to employment in the region. The technique is essential and simple, but it requires constant practice. Also, make sure that you do actually answer the question before moving on to your agenda – you are not a politician!

15. Winner smells obvious trouble in the question about the builders. It can only be trouble as there is no other reason for asking a question like that. So he sidesteps it, if a little crudely, and gets on with another plug. But this time it does not work. It is a reasonable attempt to evade the question, and he has gained some thinking time, but he realises that Sharp is not going to let this one go in a hurry.

16. So this time he says who the builders are, but quickly explains, honestly and rationally, the reason for the choice. Note his initial response: in fact he does not know any more about the local construction scene than he did in the first interview, but 'It has everywhere, I'm afraid' shows much more apparent understanding and sympathy than 'Has it?'

17. Now he is painting a picture for the viewer again and starting, in effect, to describe what his new plant will look like.

18. Sharp has interrupted again, but she also happens to be changing the subject, which is just what Winner wants. So this time he lets her.

19. Do not look a gift horse in the mouth! If a straight answer gets the key message over, then give a straight answer.
20. It is not much of a rejoinder but he has got to be quick. At least he points out that Foxtooth will get its eggs, and he spoils Sharp's snide little wind-up.

Just by using a few rules, a few techniques, all of them very simple, yet with a bit of preparation and practice, the same person achieves a vast improvement. One thing which does not show in a transcript is sincerity. This time round Winner has scored several points, but it is important to avoid being smug or snide when winning. It can be tempting to sit back with a satisfied smile, but this must be avoided at all costs.

Once the interview has been wound up the interviewee should remain sitting, looking at the interviewer, until someone tells them it is over. Even then, don't drop your guard until out of their company altogether.

CHECKLIST

PREPARATION

1. Let them do all the fussing:
   - show you to your seat;
   - fix microphone, etc;
   - ask them questions.

2. Last check on clothing:
   - stray hair;
   - straighten tie, shirt, etc;
   - pull down coat at back.

APPEARANCE AND MANNER

1. Sit up.
2. Look at interviewer throughout.
3. Speak clearly and distinctly.
4. Use hands if you wish, and do not be afraid of mannerisms, but avoid fussy or nervous movements.

---

5. Have notes if you prefer, but do not read from them.
6. Be sincere and enthusiastic throughout.

HANDLING THE INTERVIEW

Platinum rule
>   Get the key points across to the viewer, regardless of the questions and other distractions.

Golden rules
1. Do not let the interviewer butt in without a fight.
2. Refute any incorrect statements.
3. Stay off the defensive.
4. Do not get sidetracked.
5. Be positive.

Silver rules
1. Look alert.
2. Try to anticipate surprises.
3. Let the viewer know about surprises.
4. Do not address the interviewer by name.
5. If the interviewer rephrases your statements, make sure he or she has got them right.
6. Do not use jargon.
7. Remember there is only one viewer.
8. Avoid too many 'wells...'.
9. Do not fill embarrassing silences. That is the interviewer's job.
10. Stay off the 'ums' and 'ers'.
11. Do not tail off with 'and so on', 'and so forth'.
12. Only hesitate if it is deliberate.
13. Know the facts.
14. Do not get angry.
15. Do not volunteer irrelevant information.
16. Watch for the interviewer getting in a harmful last word.

17

Fine-tuning: handling different interviews

We have already looked at how programmes can vary. Most are just looking for some colour and will only become hostile if they do not get it.

But there are also one or two consumer and investigative programmes for which, on the business side of the fence, the organisations are presumed guilty before the start and some unsavoury techniques are employed to prove it.

All programmes should be treated with caution; and thorough preparation should be made. There are also some different types of interview and it is worth taking a brief look at the differences:

LIVE

Relatively few interviews are live – but they should be welcomed. The knowledge that it is for real can enhance a performance. It also guarantees that nothing can be lost or misinterpreted in subsequent editing.

RECORDED

Most interviews are recorded – but treat them just as though they were live. The first take is almost always the best. (This is also why the device of countering a pause with a pause still works on recorded interviews – the pressure on the interviewer is almost as strong as in a live one.) However, if you muck it up in the first take, you can stop and ask them to do it again – especially if they do something offside, such as introduce new evidence.

PANEL

This is where there is more than one person being interviewed – sometimes a whole studio audience. Obviously, the more interviewees the fewer messages will come across from each. The most important message must be crystal clear and in the front of your mind.

By being more interesting and colourful than the rest and not being afraid to step in if the occasion warrants, individuals can steer the odds in their favour. The director is also looking for movement, so a judicious leaning forward or the pointing of a pen or finger can help.

DOWN-THE-LINE

This is where an interviewee is in a studio in town A and is being interviewed by someone in town B. At first it can be very distracting as there is no one to talk with – just a disembodied voice and the self-consciousness of talking into a camera.

The best tip for a down-the-line interview, apart from getting used to it with practice, is to remember that talking via a microphone and a speaker with someone unseen is done every day on the telephone!

Down-the-line and 'VJ' (ie video journalist – one person both interviewing and holding the camera) interviews are the only times that the interviewee may have to look into the camera.

ON SITE

Programme-makers will often come to an organisation with a camera. The techniques are just the same as for a studio, but it can feel different in some respects.

People usually feel more at ease on their own territory and perform a little better. This is particularly true if you are standing up. We usually come over more positively when standing, hence the advice to sit *up* in a seated interview. We also tend to perform better out of doors than in. But watch out for the position of the camera. They will usually be looking for the most attractive or relevant backdrop, but it is not unknown for the 'villains' to position someone carefully in front of the factory's only chimney when it is belching black smoke, or beside a drum of chemicals with a skull and crossbones on it.

Afterwards they will often do things like 'noddies' (getting the interviewee and/or the interviewer to sit there showing silent interest in the other person's comments and questions) or re-filming the interviewer asking the questions. These are not tricks. They are simply devices to give them 'cutaway' footage to avoid 'jump cuts' during editing.

DOORSTEP

In exceptional (usually controversial) circumstances they may 'doorstep' someone by appearing from nowhere and trying to throw them into an instant interview. Do not be drawn into it.

But you also cannot afford just to slam the door or run away as they will capture this on film and show it as evidence of 'guilt'. The answer is a halfway house: stating at once that you are prepared to talk – and immediately giving a good reason why it cannot be done just now (going to an urgent meeting, etc). Or if you are outside your home or offices, they could be invited in, so that they have to dismantle the equipment and set it up again – during which time some useful preparation can be done.

Programme-makers' own official guidelines tell them that they cannot doorstep unless they have already had a reasonable request for a normal interview turned down.

IDEAS FOR PROGRAMMES

Some PR managers and consultancies are very good at exploiting the power of television – but many have yet to make the most of it. True, TV is hard to get on to because of the relatively small number of programmes compared to the print media. And it does require a degree of sophistication beyond simply sending a release and the brainless follow-up call ('Did you get our press release?').

But a little thought, imagination and persistence can do wonders. Watching programmes can give clues to the criteria for an interesting programme or news item. For a start, something has to be original. It needs to be a new development or something which is being shown for the first time. If the subject is familiar, then it requires a new insight into what goes on behind the scenes.

It must be informative. People often like to feel they are being educated and increasing their knowledge of the world about them. It must have good visual content. The viewer wants to *see* something new, not just hear it. And above all it must be entertaining. The harshest enemies of responsible business presentation on television are the other channels. It only takes the flick of a switch to leave the breathtaking excitement of the moulding shop at the Mickey Mouse Machine Tool Company and change to football or a good western.

Take a building company, for example. The camera crews will not come rushing to the builder's yard to film piles of bricks and timber and interview them proudly expounding on their profit figures. But it is another story if on one of the sites they are sinking piles to build houses on what was once useless swamp, or trying out a new building material or a new design. Almost every company has something, somewhere, at some time, that is original and interesting enough to appeal to a television programme.

The next step is to choose the target carefully and approach the right programme for the particular story. Even then it will still be a pretty random process. The most seasoned public relations professionals can never understand why sometimes a great story gets no coverage, while the next day a dead mouse under a chair will bring 20 international television crews rushing to the scene. Maybe only one good concept in ten will actually become a television programme or part of one.

CONTACTS WITH TV STATIONS AND PEOPLE

Good contacts are important. Cultivating at least one person on each of the relevant programmes has three advantages:

1. Ideas can be bounced off someone who always knows what the programme is looking for.
2. An offering is more credible if the contact is known to them.
3. While never immune from the third degree, tough treatment is less likely without due warning.

Very few television people are as snotty as they are made out to be, and despite the glamour and remoteness of television they are really only journalists underneath – and journalists love new contacts. Breaking the ice should take no more than a phone call. Look up the name of the editor and producer, etc in the media directories or get a copy of the *Blue Book of British Broadcasting* (Tellex Monitors Ltd). Or ring the switchboard of the programme or production company.

By thinking of a couple of reasons why the programme-makers should be interested in the idea, success is not guaranteed but at least is more likely. These people are professionals and are always looking for new leads.

The editor is the key figure, but will be very busy. The producer is a useful contact, too, but do not overlook the humble researcher. Researchers are the worker ants who go out and do all the delving for the editor or producer. They sift through the newspaper clippings and stories from all sorts of sources, looking for material for the next programme.

Business and PR people lavish less attention on them than on editors and producers, yet the programme-makers attach more importance to a story which comes from the researcher (and maybe planted by you) than one which you try to flog direct.

VIDEO NEWS RELEASES

It is also worth considering a VNR (video news release), where a specialist company makes a mini-programme and distributes it to the TV stations (or as syndicated audio tapes to the radio stations) in broadcast-quality format. It is the TV equivalent of a press release.

There are mixed views on the efficiency of these. Some VNRs have had spectacular success because they fulfil the various criteria of being colourful, relevant, interesting, etc. Many, if not most, go straight into the plastic recycling bin.

They can also be very expensive, so they require careful discussion and planning with a specialist VNR company – and a healthy whiff of scepticism.

18

How: radio interviews

On radio the listener is practically sitting there saying: 'Come on, what have you got to tell me?' In contrast, the television viewer is sitting there like an overfed Roman consul saying: 'Amuse me.'

Radio journalists may slip the old knuckle-dusters on from time to time, but in general radio tends to be more concerned with interesting the listener than with crucifying the interviewee. This can require even more concentration. But at least interviewees usually get a fair hearing on radio.

Local stations are generally run on a shoestring, so with a limited reporting staff they are delighted to have people come to them with material. Is a local organisation expanding? Cutting down? Fighting the council over something? Do they have a new product? Are they organising a charity function? Making a profit? A loss? Creating (or cutting) jobs? Local radio will take material that a national station would not look at – so long as it is of local interest, and especially if it makes an attention-grabbing noise.

RADIO INTERVIEW TECHNIQUES

The techniques for radio interviews are basically similar to those for television, but there are a few important differences.

Preparation

The decision on whether to do the interview or not and the information required from the producers is the same as with TV (see Chapter 15). The preparation must be just as painstaking and thorough. Stick to two or three key points, with three or four subpoints for each. Anecdotes are, if anything, even more crucial. A short story, a parable, a brief tale of success or disaster – the radio listener will lap it up.

The same goes for the analogies. The television viewer expects to be shown a picture of something all the time, but the radio listener has to paint his or her own mental pictures.

A good example of creating an image in the listener's mind was the radio presenter who interviewed an expert on hayfever, and looking down a microscope at a speck of pollen, said, 'It looks like a tennis ball stuffed with semolina!'

The studio

Radio stations are generally smaller than television ones, and interviewees usually sit at a table with a microphone right in front of them. Surprisingly, a radio studio can be more distracting than a TV one. The sound-proofing is often more noticeable and, unlike their TV counterparts, radio interviewers might be changing CDs and doing other things instead of looking at the interviewee when he or she is talking.

Voice test

Voice tests are conducted for the same reason as on television. Interviewees should speak at the level they intend to use for the rest of the interview. Unlike television, the microphone cannot be ignored.

Manner

It is still a good idea to sit up or forward in the chair, because it is important to be alert and in command of things. It is even more important to speak clearly and distinctly. On television the viewer is able to do a spot of lip-reading to aid comprehension, but the radio listener can only hear the voice.

It is much easier on radio to refer to notes for guidance. But do not read from them or rustle the paper.

Sincerity, enthusiasm

This is where radio starts to get difficult. In front of a camera there are two ways of demonstrating enthusiasm and sincerity – facial expressions and tone of voice. But the microphone only picks up the latter, so this has to convey everything. The listener has not heard your voice before, so the speaker should sound interested and excited.

Listening to the radio will give clues to why some interviewers succeed and others do not. Good radio interviewers are as good at their job as any television interviewer, and will keep things moving and interrupt if the interviewee starts to waffle.

TYPES OF INTERVIEW

The interview types are pretty much the same as television, but some special handling is required for some of them.

Panel

Groups of experts, or people who disagree with one another, come over well on radio. The trouble is that it is harder to get attention. There is no director to turn the camera on a speaker, so participants have to speak out at the right moment and be that little bit more forceful.

Down-the-line

This is not easy. In a down-the-line radio interview the interviewee sits there in solitary confinement, totally remote from the interviewer and any other participants. Remember the tip from Chapter 17 about pretending to be on the phone.

Telephone

The telephone gives radio producers an easy means of interviewing all sorts of people at short notice, at any time of the day, and in any location. It is also a popular way of obtaining the view of the general public on phone-in programmes.

Used properly, the telephone can provide a good avenue to get the information across. All that is required is some preparation beforehand and the right kind of handling.

At home or at the office, the speaker can choose how to sit and which room to use. They are on their own territory, which is a psychological advantage. As with any interview outside the studio, avoiding interruptions is important. If in the office, incoming calls should go to someone else. At home, shut the doors and send the kids to the park – with the dog. A busy road or other noise source should be out of earshot. It is essential not to listen to the interview on the radio at the same time as this can cause feedback howl.

Dealing with a 'stitch-up'

Sometimes programme-makers will consciously set you up and twist the facts to suit their case. Such an occurrence is far more rare than many critics of the media realise, but there are still one or two mildly unhinged researchers and presenters who see evil in every company, and who seek to expose their 'evil' at any cost – even that of the truth.

If you think that this might happen, the best defence is one of attack. Accept the invitation to appear, even if you know they are going to try to savage you and/or spring a surprise on you. If you follow the advice of this book, you should come out on top, but even if they still manage to stitch you up, at least the public will see your human face – someone who shows that they care and who is visibly being treated unfairly by bear-baiters. If you don't appear, then they will quite certainly stitch you up in your absence!

If you are worried that the programme could do a great deal of damage, consult, as early in the game as possible, a *specialist* PR firm and/or lawyer for advice on negotiating the minefield. There are some quite strict protections for 'victims' of misrepresentation to be found in the *ITC Code of Conduct* and the *BBC Producers' Guidelines* (available at the BBC bookshop in Portland Place, London). Also, the broadcast watchdog, Ofcom, investigates complaints about unfair treatment.

Conclusion

Used correctly, the media is an invaluable tool for the public relations practitioner. The professional should be aware of how the development of the media has affected its willingness and ability to cover issues. The fast pace of technological change means it is imperative to keep up with the new media and understand how to use them. Indeed, many believe that in the future all contact will be via electronic means such as e-mail and the internet, rendering the need for printed media obsolete. The increasing range of broadcast media may mean that, while getting on to television may become easier as the number of outlets increases, effective presentation and targeting will become more important to reach the relevant public.

This book is only the beginning for the professional. Background and techniques can only have limited use in a book. What is needed is for the serious public relations practitioner to get out there and do it, and so add their own opinions and techniques to those set out here. Above all it should be remembered that public relations and the media have to work together – each would be the poorer without the other. Together, they can produce interesting and informative material, mutually beneficial to both the client or employer organisation and the newspaper or broadcast.

It is hoped that this book has provided some useful information in continuing to improve that relationship.

Further reading

BOOKS AND PAMPHLETS

BBC, *Extending Choice*, BBC, 1992

Belsey and Chadwick (eds), *Ethical Issues in Journalism and the Media*, 1992

Bland, M, *When It Hits the Fan*, Centre Publishing, 2004

Cunningham, J, *Cable TV*, Howard Sans and Co, 1976

Curran, J and Seaton, J, *Power Without Responsibility: The press and broadcasting in Britain*, 4th edn, Routledge, 1994

Fairchild, M, *Research and Evaluation Toolkit*, CIPR/PRCA, 1999

Greenwood, W and Welsh, T, *McNae's Essential Law for Journalists*, 12th edn, Butterworths, 1992

IRP, *Public Relations and the Law*, IRP, 1994

Jenkins, S, *Newspapers: The power and the money*, Faber and Faber, 1979

Rush, J, *The Death of Spin?* CIPR/PRCA, 2000

Smith, A, *Subsidies and the Press in Europe*, PEP, 1977

Snoddy, R, *The Good, the Bad and the Unacceptable*, Faber and Faber, 1992

Theaker, A, *The PR Handbook*, Routledge, 2004

Thomas, R, *Broadcasting and Democracy in France*, Bradford University Press, 1976

Williams, A, *Broadcasting and Democracy in West Germany*, Bradford University Press, 1976

Williams, G *Britain's Media – How They are Related*, CPBF, 1994

BROADCASTS

BBC 2, *Money Programme* (Rupert Murdoch), 21 May 1995
  Close up North (Gold Diggers) 23 March 1995

Channel 4, *Satellite Wars*, 26 March 1995, 2 April 1995, 9 April 1995
  Daily Planet, 19 March 1995
  Whole World in His Hands, March 1995
  Naked News, 23 March 1995

ARTICLES

Anglesey, Lady, 'Watchdog firmly on a Legislative Leash', *Guardian*, 4 November 1995

Arden, Z, 'Open Road', *PR Week*, 17 March 1995

Downey, G, 'Press Regulation', *Independent*, 16 November 1992

Fitzwalter, R, 'Tales wag the Watchdog', *Guardian*, 14 October 1991

Fountain, N, 'A Splash of Colour', *Guardian*, 5 December 1994

Gray, R, 'Murdoch Outflanked', *PR Week*, 2 June 1995

Katz, J, 'Tomorrow's Word', *Guardian*, 24 April 1995

Mullin, C, 'Regulations to Save the Nation', *Journalist*, February/ March 1995

Murdoch, R, 'Cross? You Bet!', *Guardian*, 29 May 1995

Stott, R, 'Naked Power', *Guardian*, 11 January 1993

Sweeting, A, 'Rolling on and on', *Guardian*, 5 December 1994

Index

Acts of Parliament
  Broadcasting (1990)   13, 25
  Broadcasting (1996)   32
  Cable and Broadcasting   34
  Communications (2003)   13, 23
  Contempt of Court   15, 17
  Freedom of Information (2000)   17
  Freedom of Information (Scotland)
    (2002)   17
  Independent Broadcasting Authority
    (IBA) (1973)   19
  Official Secrets   17
advertising, TV   94
advertorial   39, 53, 60–62, 78
Altavista   36
America   see United States of America
    (USA)
Associated Newspapers   12, 13, 35
AT&T   36
Australian, The   12

BBC   see British Broadcasting Corporation
BBC Producers' Guidelines   137
Blue Book of Broadcasting   131
Boston Globe   20
Boston Herald   12
British Broadcasting Corporation   7, 22,
    29–30, 32, 39
  current roles   29

Davies review (1999)   29
digital radio services   32
Extending Choice (1992)   29
funding, the future   29
government review process   29–30
licence-fee funding   29, 30
National Heritage Select Committee   29
quality of programmes   29
Reith, John   7
Royal Charter   7, 19, 26, 29
Today programme   22
websites   29 *see also main entry*
World Service   33
British Media Industry Group   13
British Telecom   34–35, 36
broadcast coverage   93–96
  proactive television   94–96
  as public relations tool   94
  radio   94
  TV advertising   94
broadcast media   91–137
  coverage, importance of   see broadcast
    coverage
  interviews, handling different   see main
    entry
  interview, winning the   see main entry
  preparation/briefing   see broadcast
    media: preparation/briefing
  radio interviews   see main entry

broadcast media: preparation/briefing
   97–107
   brevity 99
   familiarity 101
   impact 100
   interview, preparing for a TV 102–05
      see also main entry
   journalists 101
   knowing the brief 101
   planning the message 98–99
   questions and considerations 97–98
   questions, listing likely 101–02
   relevance 101
   repetition 100
   simplicity 99–100
broadcasting codes of conduct 17
broadcasting in the UK 7, 25–30
   BBC *see* British Broadcasting
      Corporation
   consequences for 29
   franchise battle 25–26 *see also*
      franchise(s)
   ITV, future of 27–28 *see also* television
      companies
   PR in franchise battle 26–27 *see also*
      franchise(s)
   PR in ITV, future of 28
Broadcasting Standards Commission (BSC)
   see Ofcom
Broadcasting Standards Council
BT *see* British Telecom

Cable and Broadcasting Act (1974) *see also*
   cable television
Cable Authority 34 *see also* cable
   television
Cable News Network 33
cable television 34–35 *see also* satellite
   television *and* television companies
   advantages for providers 35
   Channel One 35
   companies
      ntl 34, 35, 36
      Telewest 35, 36
   cross-media, benefits of 34
   fibre-optic cables/interactive systems
      34
   France *see main entry*
   franchises 34–35
   pay-TV systems 35
   programme quality 35
Calcutt Committee (1990) 19–20,
   21–22
Campbell, Alastair 23
CARMA International 41
Carnival cruises 58–59

checklist for effective press relations
   87–89
   advance warning 87, 88
   audience-angled stories 87
   brochures 88
   contact names 88
   deadlines 87
   embargoes 88
   photographs 88, 89
   quotes 88
   stereotypes, avoiding 89
   timing 88
   up-to-date contact lists 87
   website 88, 89
CIPR *see* Public Relations, Chartered
   Institute of
CNN *see* Cable News Network
codes of conduct 16–17
   broadcasting 17
   Ofcom (formerly Broadcasting Standards
      Commission) 17
   NUJ 16
   Press Complaints Commission 16–17
computerised typesetting 11
conferences/receptions, press *see* press
   conferences/receptions
copyright, photographers' 71
Council of Europe 12
   'Concentration of media ownership and
      its impact on media freedom and
      pluralism' 12
customer confidentiality 81

Daily Express 10
Daily Herald 6
Daily Mail 10, 12, 35
Daily Mirror 10
Daily Star 22
Daily Telegraph, The 10, 13, 48
Davies review (1999) 29 *see also* British
   Broadcasting Corporation
DBS *see* Direct Broadcasting by Satellite
dealing with the press 45–89 *see also*
   individual subject entries
   checklist for effective press relations
      78–89
   features 68–69, 76–77
   news 66–68
   newspapers/periodicals 47–54
   photographs/photography 65, 69–70,
      76
   press agencies 51–52
   press relations 55–64
   talking to the press 79–85
   writing for the press 73–78
defamation 16

digital broadcasting/television 35–36
  availability of channels 35
  ending of analogue service 35
Direct Broadcasting by Satellite 32 *see also*
  satellite television
directories, media 53
Dow Jones Interactive (press coverage)
  42–43
down-the-line 128–29, 135–36
Dyke, Greg 23, 29

e-mail 36, 74
Echo Research 42
editorial integrity 64
editors
  Elias, Julias (Lord Southwood) 10
  MacKenzie, Kelvin 21
  as useful contacts 131
embargoes 75, 80, 88
ethics and privacy 19–23 *see also* France;
  Germany *and* United States of
  America (USA)
  Calcutt Committee (1990) 19–20, 21–22
  Hutton enquiry 23
  Independent Broadcasting Authority
    (IBA) Act (1973) 19
  Neill Committee 22
  Nolan Committee 22
  Press Complaints Commission 22
  privacy of individual(s) 21–22
  Private Members' Bills 21
  regulation 21–23
  Royal Charter, BBC 19
Europe: broadcasting/press in *see* media
  history
evaluation *see* media evaluation
Evening Standard 10
Express, The 6, 10

Fahrenheit 9/11 21
Fair Trading, Office of 26
Fairchild, M 43
features 68–69, 76–77 *see also*
  photographs *and* PR features
  advertising, as vehicle for 68
  handling journalists' enquiries 76–77
  freelance writers 68
  ghosts/ghosting 68, 77
  interviews 68
  newspapers, regional and local 68
  PR-generated material 69
  product-testing 68
  think pieces 68
Federal Communications Commission
  (FCC) 13 *see also* United States of
  America (USA)

Financial Times 6, 13, 49, 51
flaming 37 *see also* internet
Fleet Street, demise of 11
  computer typesetting, cost of 11
  losses 11
  new technology 11
  print unions, power of 11
  restrictive practices 11
Flight International 53, 54
France 6, 7–8, 11–12, 20, 34
  ARTE: French/German collaboration 8
  cable television 34
  High Audiovisual Council 34
  media concentration protests 12
  media ownership rules 12
  news, control of radio and television
    7–8, 20
  newspapers 6
  Press Law (1881) 6
  radio 7
  Socpresse 12
  television channels 8
franchise(s) *see also* broadcasting in the UK
  and television companies
  bidding system 25–26
  consequences for BBC 29–30
  future of ITV 27–28
  ITV 25–26, 27–28
  lobbying campaigns 27
  PR in franchise battle 26
  press coverage 27
  public relations future in ITV 28
  quality threshold 29
  Royal Charter, BBC 26, 29–30
Freeview 32

Germany 6–7, 12
  Basic Law (1945) 8, 20
  expansion into Central and Eastern
    Europe 12
  foreign investment 12
  Hugenberg, Alfred 7
  media concentration, fear of 12
  Nazi control 7
  ownership, press 6–7, 12
  post-WWII press/broadcasting 7
  radio stations 8
  satellite stations 8
  Statutes Movement 20
  television channels 8
ghosts/ghosting 68, 77
Glasgow Media Unit 22
Google 36
Green Paper (1995) 13
Grocer, The 53, 54
Guardian, The 6, 13, 50

IBA   *see* Independent Broadcasting
   Authority
IMPACON   42
Independent Broadcasting Authority   32
Independent Television Commission   25
   Code of Conduct   137
Independent, The   11
India TV
   cable   33
   Doorshana   33
Integrated Systems Digital Network (ISDN)
   32, 36
internet   36–37 *see also* technology, new
   media
   audio and video clips   36
   broadband   36
   e-mail   36
   flaming   37
   as information source   36–37
   ISDN   36
   Joint Academic Network (JANET)   36
   journalists, use by   36
   music, applications for   36
   netiquette   37
   press releases   37
   search engines   36 *see also main entry*
   viruses   37
   World Wide Web   36, 37
Internet Commission (CIPR/PRCA)
   37–38
interview, preparing for a   102–05
   bridging from question to message
      103–04
   checklist   105
   clothes and make-up   104–05
   final brief: example   106
   natural communication   104
   nerves: helpful tips   102–03
   positive thinking   103
   rehearsing   103
   relating to interviewer   105
   warm-up   102
interview, winning the TV   109–25
   checklist   124–25
   dos and don'ts   109–10
   good interview: getting message across
      118–24
   key points   117
   poor interview: example   110
interviews, handling different   127–32
   doorstep   29–30
   down-the-line   128–29
   live   127–28
   on site   129
   panel   128
   programme ideas   130–31

recorded   128
   useful contacts   131
   video news releases (VNRs)   131–32
interviews, press   *see* press interviews
interviews, radio   *see* radio interviews
Iraq war   23
ISDN *see* Integrated Systems Digital
   Network
ITC Code of Conduct   137
ITV   22, 25-26, 27-28

JANET *see* Joint Academic Network
jargon   80–81
   deadline   81
   embargo   80 *see also* embargoes
   no comment   80
   non-attributable   80
   off the record   80
   on the record   80
   quote   80
   scoop   81
Joint Academic Network (JANET)   36
journalists   2, 79–80, 81, 101
   lunching with   82
   at press conferences   84
   as useful contacts   131
Journalists, International Federation of   12
Journalists, National Union of   5
   Code of Conduct   5, 16

Le Figaro   12
Lexis Nexis press coverage system   42–43
libel   15–16
Living   48
Lloyds List   53, 66
London Daily News   11
Los Angeles Times   11
lunching with journalists   82

MAC   *see* multiple analogue component
   system
Mail on Sunday   12
mailing lists   76
media content analysis   41–42
   CARMA International   41
   Echo Research   42
   IMPACON   42
   Media Measurement Ltd/i-sight   41
media corporations   *see also* media
   ownership
   Associated Newspapers   12, 13
   Disney   13
   EMAP   12
   Fox   13
   Harmsworth House (USA)   12
   Herald-Sun TV (Australia)   12

Mirror Group   9, 11
News International   9, 12
Pearson   13
Thomson Regional Newspapers   50
Tribune (USA)   13
United Newspapers   9
Viacom   12, 13
media evaluation   39–43
   coverage v content   42–43
      impact on business   43
      press coverage systems   42–43
      public opinion   43
      setting objectives   43
   media content analysis   41–42 *see main
      entry*
   methods of evaluation   39
   research   40–41 *see also* research, media
      evaluation
Media Evaluation Companies, Association
   of (AMEC)   42 *see also* websites
media history   5–8 *see also* British
   Broadcasting Corporation
   Alexandra Palace   7
   commercial television (UK)   7
   Europe, broadcasting in   7–8 *see also*
      France *and* Germany
   Europe, the press in   6–7 *see also* France
      and Germany
   United Kingdom   7
media law   15–18
   broadcasting codes   17 *see also* codes of
      conduct
   codes of conduct   16–17 *see also main
      entry*
   contempt of court   15
   defamation   16
   libel and slander   15–16
   media reform   16–18 *see also* Acts of
      Parliament
media ownership   9–14
   concentration of   9, 17
   cross-media ownership 12–13 *see also*
      media corporations *and* newspaper
      proprietors
   Fleet Street, demise of   11 *see also main
      entry*
   France and Germany   11–12 *see also*
      France *and* Germany
   future development   13–14
   online press   13
   personalities/papers   9–10 *see also*
      newspaper proprietors
media technology   *see* technology, new
   media
Modern Railways   53
Moore, Michael   21

multiple analogue component system
   32–33

National Heritage Select Committee (1993)
National News Council   20
Neill Committee   22
netiquette   37
New York Post (USA)   11
news   65–68 *see also* features *and*
   photographs
   content   66
   examples of   66
   objectivity   66
   photographs   65–66
   reader, appeal to   67
   regional/local circulation areas   67
   timing of   67–68
News of the World, The   12, 22
News on Sunday   11
newspaper companies/corporations   *see*
   media corporations
newspaper proprietors   9–10, 23
   Aitken, Max (Lord Beaverbrook)   10
   Astor, Colonel   10
   Astor, William Waldorf   10
   Black, Conrad   10
   Dassault, Marcel   12
   Hearst, William Randolph   9–10
   Hersant, Robert   11
   King, Cecil Harmsworth   10
   Maxwell, Robert   10, 21
   Murdoch, Rupert   10, 11, 13–14, 21, 32
   Newnes, George   10
   Northcliffe, Lord (Alfred Harmsworth)
      10
   Rothermere, Lord (Harold Harmsworth)
      10
   Shah, Eddie   11
   Thomson, Roy   10
newspapers/periodicals   47–54
   consumer periodicals   52–53, 63
      advertorial   53
      county magazines   52
      supermarket sales   53, 63
      women's interest   48, 52
   general press   48–49
   local press   50–51, 60
      community   51
      freesheets   50, 51
      paid for   50
      staffing   51
      unpaid contributors   51
   London papers   50
   national/regional press   49–50, 59
      advertising revenue   50
      evening papers   49

news coverage 49–50
staffing 50
press agencies 51–52 *see also main entry*
specialised periodicals 53–54
academic 54
content 53
directories 53
format 53
frequency of publication 53–54
staffing 54
standards 54
targeting 47–48
Nolan Committee (1995) 22
Northern Star 5
NUJ *see* Journalists, National Union of

Ofcom 17, 23, 137
Code of Practice 17

PA *see* Press Association
PAL *see* phase alternate line
PCC *see* Press Complaints Commission
Periodical Publishers' Association 62
Petit Journal 6
phase alternate line 33
photocomposition 11
photographic checklist 70–71
photographs/photography 65–66, 69–70, 76
client needs, advice on 69–70
colour 65, 69, 70
copyright 71
cost 70
media requirements 70
news/picture agencies 70
stereotypes, avoiding 69
tailoring to audience 69
Political Register 10
PR features 77–78 *see also* features
advertorial 78
advice pieces 78
company products, reviews of 78
ghosting 77
review pieces 78
rules 78
PR Planner 53
PR Week 40
PRCA *see* Public Relations Consultants Association
press, dealing with the *see* dealing with the press
press agencies 51–52
AP-Dow Jones 52
overseas 52
photographers 52
PR consultancies

Reuters 51
types of 51–52
UPI 52
Press Association 51
Press and Broadcasting Freedom, Campaign for 17
Press Complaints Commission 16–17, 22
Code of Practice 17
website 17
press conferences/receptions 83–85
advantages of 83–84
investment analysts, inviting 84
journalists, meeting informally 84
organising, main points in 84–85
rehearsals 84
timing of 84, 85
website, conference material on 85
Press Council 22
press interviews 82–83
as briefing for PR function 83
press officers 83
public relations (PR) practitioner 83
timing 82–83
press relations 55–64
editorial integrity 64
effective, checklist for 87–89 *see also* checklist for effective press relations
employee attitudes 56
employee communications programmes 56
matching the media *see* press relations: matching the media
media relations 56
PR managers/consultancies
product promotion *see also* press relations: product promotion
public relations, reasons for using 55–56
public relations vs paid-for editorial 64
quality of 56
press relations: matching the media 57–60
audiences 57–58
effective use of media 59–60
function 57
messages 58–59
reader-enquiry cards 59
press relations: product promotion 60–63
advertorial 60–62
colour separation charges 62
promotional offers 62–63
reader competitions 62
self-financing offers 62–63
sponsorship 63
press releases 1, 73–75
accuracy 74
concluding 75

dating 74
e-mail 74
embargoes 75 *see also main entry*
failure, reasons for 74
first paragraph, importance of 74
headlines 74
jargon 74 *see also main entry*
layout 74
length 74
paragraph lengths 74
photographs 75
phrases to avoid 74
product samples 75
quotes 74
research, time for 75
style 74
targeting 74
versions of 75
print unions 11
producers as useful contacts 131
Public Relations, Chartered Institute of
   22–23, 37, 40
   Code of Practice 23
   Internet Commission 37–38
   task force: CIPR/PRCA 40
Public Relations Consultants Association
   22–23, 37, 40
   Code of Practice 23
   Internet Commission 37–38
   task force: CIPR/PRCA 40
public relations (PR) 1–2, 43, 52, 55–56, 64
   in ITV 28
   practitioners 1–2, 38, 83

radio 7, 31–32, 94
   digital services 32
   local 133
   news 7–8, 20
   stations 8
radio broadcasting companies/stations
   31–32
   Classic FM 12, 31
   community stations 31–32
   digital broadcasting 32
   Digital One 32
   Great Western Radio 12, 32
   ISDN 32
   Talk Radio 31
   Virgin 31
radio interviews 133–37
   down-the-line 135–36
   enthusiasm 135
   interesting the listener 133, 134
   local radio 133
   manner 135
   panel 135

preparation for 134
sincerity 135
studio 134
telephone 136
unfair tactics 136–37
voice tests 134
reader-enquiry cards 59
receptions, press *see*
   conferences/receptions, press
research, media evaluation 40–41 *see also*
   media evaluation
   advertising value equivalents (AVE) 41
   audience attitudes 40
   before-and-after 40
   CIPR/PRCA task force 40
   communications audit 40
   MORI 40
   PR%f campaign/Toolkit 40–41
   pre- and post-campaign 40
   tracking studies 40
research
   RAJAR (2003) 32
   Which? online internet survey 37
researchers as useful contacts 131
Reuters 51

San Francisco Examiner 9
satellite television 32–34
   Asiasat 32
   Astra 33
   British Satellite Broadcasting (BSB)
      32–33
   Eutelsat 32
   Freeview 34
   multiple analogue component system
      (MAC) 32–33
   ntl 34, 35, 36
   phase alternate line (PAL) 33
   Sky Television 32–34, 36
   Star TV 33
   Telewest 34, 35, 36
   Telstar 32
   Zee TV 33
Scotsman, The 75
Scottish Daily Express 49
Scottish Daily Mail 49
Scottish Daily Mirror 49
Scottish Sun 49
search engines 36 *see also* internet
Sky Television 13, 32–34, 36
   Moviemax 33
   Sky Channel 33
   Sky Sport 33
slander 15–16
Spectator, The xi
spin doctoring 37–38

Sun, The   10, 12, 21
Sunday Correspondent   11
Sunday Express   10
Sunday Sport   21, 22
Sunday Telegraph   xi
Sunday Times, The   1, 12, 15, 64

talking to the press   79–85
  conferences/receptions   83–85 *see also*
    press conferences/receptions
  customer confidentiality   81
  interviews   82–83 *see also* press
    interviews
  jargon   80–81 *see also main entry*
  journalists   79–80, 81
  journalists/PR practitioners, relationship
    between   81
  lunching/theme lunches   82
technology, new media   31–38
  cable television   34–35 *see also main entry*
  digital broadcasting   32, 35–36
  heat-set colour   31
  internet   36–37 *see also main entry*
  radio   31–32 *see also* British Broadcasting
    Corporation *and* radio broadcasting
    companies/stations
  satellite television   32–34 *see also main*
    entry
  spin doctoring: the future   37–38
    Internet Commission   37–38
    PR practitioners, opportunity for   38
television companies   25–26 *see also* cable
    television *and* satellite television
  Anglia   26, 28
  Border 226
  Carlton   26, 27, 28
  Central   26, 28
  Channel 4   27
  Channel Islands   26, 28
  Grampian   26, 28
  Granada   26, 28
  HTV   26, 28
  ITC   27
  ITV   28
  ITV Digital   28
  LWT   26, 28
  Media   28
  Meridian   26, 27
  ONDigital   28
  Scottish/Scottish Media   26, 28
  STV   28
  Sunrise   26
  Thames   26, 27
  TSW   26
  TV-AM   26

TVS   26, 27
Tyne Tees   26, 28
Ulster   26, 28
United News   28
Westcountry   12, 26, 28
Yorkshire   26, 28
YTV   26–27, 28
television personnel as useful contacts
    131
Tellex Monitors   131
Times Mirror   13
Times, The   6, 10, 12, 51, 64
Today   11
TV advertising   *see* advertising, TV
Two Ten Communications   37, 52

UKGold   35
United States of America (USA)
  Bush government   21
  cable television   34
  CNN   35
  court proceedings, coverage of   20
  ethics   20
  Federal Communications Commission
    13, 34
  First Amendment   20
  Hutchins Commission (1947)   20
  media behaviour   20–21
  media concentration   17
  media ownership   13
  National News Council   20
  pro-government news coverage   21
  television ownership   13
USA   *see* United States of America (USA)
useful contacts   131

video news release (VNR)   131–32
viruses   *see* internet

Wall Street Journal   51
website(s)   76
Western Morning News   43
Westminster Press   10
Which?   66
  online internet survey   37
World Wide Web   36, 37 *see also* internet
writing for the press   73–78
  distribution   76
  features   76–77 *see also main entry*
  mailing lists   76
  PR features   77–78 *see also main entry*
  press releases   73   *also main entry*
  websites   76

Yahoo   36